Millbrook Kids' Fair

MILLBROOK
TOWN

First published in the United Kingdom in 2025 by Millbrook Education Ltd.

ISBN: 978-1-9194356-0-2

www.millbrooktown.co.uk

For EMS, Amble Pamble,

and Marchie-Moo.

Contents

Chapter 1 Parent/Educator Guide

Concept: Scarcity

All resources (e.g. money, time, energy, materials, people) are limited. When we can't have everything we want, we face scarcity and must make choices.

In a Child's World

Children experience scarcity when choosing between activities ("I can only go to one birthday party"), managing pocket money, or sharing limited resources with siblings. They're already making economic decisions; this book helps them recognise the pattern.

In Your World

You face the same principle when budgeting household expenses, allocating time between work and family, or deciding between competing priorities. The economic concept is identical; only the scale changes.

Why it Matters

Understanding scarcity is about making thoughtful choices. Children who recognise resource constraints early become creative problem-solvers who maximise what they have rather than focusing on what they lack.

1

'Good' Ideas

Maya's hands were shaking as she climbed the ladder. Not from the effort, she'd made this climb hundreds of times, but from the crumpled paper stuffed in her back pocket. The paper that was about to ruin everything.

"Finally!" Connor's head appeared over the edge of the treehouse. "We've been waiting ages. Jamal's on his seventh biscuit."

"It's science," Jamal called from inside. "I'm timing structural failure in tea. Forty-three seconds, if anyone's interested."

"Nobody's interested," Connor said cheerfully, reaching down to help Maya up the last bit.

The treehouse was their place. Four mismatched cushions around a cable-reel table, fairy lights wound through the rafters, a crooked shelf holding biscuits and the notebook labelled OFFICIAL CREW BUSINESS in Maya's determined handwriting. Normally, being here made everything feel manageable.

Today, nothing felt manageable.

"What's wrong?" Lily asked immediately. She'd set down her sketchbook, her eyes already worried.

The others noticed too. Connor stopped mid-chew. Jamal's eyebrows drew together in the way they did when he was calculating something.

Maya pulled the paper from her pocket. She'd grabbed it from the recycling bin after her mum threw it away. Now she smoothed it out on the table, pressing down the creases with her palm.

MILLBROOK TOWN COUNCIL: PUBLIC NOTICE
Annual Millbrook Community Fair: **CANCELLED**

For a long moment, nobody spoke.

"Cancelled?" Connor's voice cracked. "They can't just... cancel it."

"They can," Jamal stared at his hands. "They did."

Lily picked up the paper, reading it again as though the words might rearrange themselves into something less terrible. "But the fair's been going forever. My mum went when she was little. Her mum went when she was little."

"My gran went when she was my age." Maya's voice came out steadier than she felt. "She talks about it all the time. The carousel with the painted horses. The coconut shy. The sticky toffee apples that pulled your fillings out." She tried to smile but couldn't quite manage it. "She was going to take me to see the horses this year."

The treehouse felt smaller suddenly, the afternoon light through the windows less golden than before.

"Budget constraints," Jamal read from the notice.

"Brilliant," Connor muttered. "So they've got no money and we've got no fair."

"There's more," Maya said.

She pulled out a second piece of paper, this one neatly printed on council letterhead. "I went to the council meeting. Last night..."

Three faces stared blankly at her.

"You went to a council meeting?" Connor looked as though she'd announced a trip to the moon. "On purpose?"

"My mum was going anyway. They were discussing the cancellation. I sat at the back." Maya could still feel the uncomfortable plastic chair, still smell the staleness of the community hall. "Councillor Davies, you know, the one with the moustache who's always complaining about parking. He was arguing with everyone. Saying the fair's too expensive, a waste of money, that council should focus on 'real priorities.'"

"Sounds like Councillor Davies," Jamal said. "My dad calls him Harold the Grump."

"But then Mrs. Sharma stood up. Our Mrs. Sharma, from school." Maya paused, remembering the headteacher's calm, clear voice cutting through the bickering. "She asked him to think about how disappointed the children would be if the fair was cancelled."

Lily leaned forward. "What happened?"

"Councillor Davies laughed at her. Said children don't know the first thing about these decisions." Maya's jaw tightened. "He said if kids understood anything about money, they'd know we couldn't afford the fair."

Nobody seemed to know what to say.

"And then," Maya continued, "Mrs. Sharma said something I can't stop thinking about. She said: 'Perhaps the children could show us all something about making good choices. Perhaps if they can run even a small event successfully, it would prove that community spirit is worth investing in.'"

Connor sat up straight. "A small event?"

"She called it a Kids' Fair. Just for one afternoon. Not the whole big fair, something smaller. Something we could plan and run ourselves."

"Us?" Lily's eyes grew wider. "Plan a fair?"

"The council voted." Maya smoothed the second piece of paper on the table. "Councillor Davies only agreed because he thinks we'll fail. But they gave permission. The school field, last Saturday of term. We'd have to do everything. Plan it, run it." She looked up at her friends. "And they gave us a budget."

"How much?" Jamal asked, before Maya could fully complete her sentence.

"£200."

The number hung in the air.

"Two hundred quid for a whole fair?" Connor laughed, but it wasn't his usual happy laugh. "My dad's stall at the normal fair costs more than that just to set up."

"That's the point," Maya said. "Councillor Davies thinks we'll prove him right. That we'll realise it's impossible and give up. That kids don't understand that things cost money." She looked at each of them in turn. Jamal with his furrowed brow, Lily clutching her sketchbook, Connor already drumming his fingers absent mindedly. "But what if we proved him wrong?"

"What if we proved that a community fair can work?" Lily's voice was soft but steady. "Even a small one?"

"Exactly." Maya felt the stones in her stomach finally settling. "If we show them it's possible. If we actually pull this off, maybe they'll see that the big fair is worth saving too."

Silence stretched between them. Then Jamal pulled out his phone and opened the calculator app. Lily turned to a fresh page in her sketchbook.

"Right then," Connor said. "What do we need for a fair?"

They started with dreams.

"A bouncy castle!" Lily bounced slightly on her cushion, as though testing the concept. "Every fair needs a bouncy castle. The big ones shaped like castles, with the turrets, and the..."

"Write it down, write it down!" Connor urged.

Maya had taken charge of the Official Crew Business notebook, her pen moving fast. "Bouncy castle. What else?"

"Petting zoo." Jamal spoke with unusual enthusiasm. "With the baby goats. Remember last year? That tiny one kept trying to eat Dr Williams' tie."

"Brilliant. Petting zoo with goats." Maya added it to the list. "Connor?"

"Candy floss machine. Obviously. And one of those hook-a-duck games, you know, where you fish the ducks out and win prizes? And a coconut shy. My dad could help build that, he's got spare wood in the garage."

"Face painting!" Lily was sketching furiously now, tigers and butterflies appearing on her page. "I could do face painting. And there should be food! Hot dogs and burgers, and maybe a cake stall."

"And music," Maya added, writing faster. "Proper fair music, with the announcements. 'Will the owner of a brown goat please return to the petting zoo, it's eating another tie.'"

They laughed, the earlier gloom lifting. The list grew:

Bouncy castle (the big kind), Petting zoo (with goats), Candy floss machine, Hook-a-duck, Coconut shy, Face painting (Lily), Hot dogs/burgers, Cake stall, Live music, Balloon animals, Tombola Raffle, Guess the weight of the cake, Splat-the-rat, Welly wanging, Strongman hammer thing, Ice cream van.

"Don't forget the carousel!" Maya added, thinking of her gran. "With the painted horses."

"And one of those teacup rides," Lily suggested. "Where you spin in circles until you feel sick."

"Fortune teller booth!" Connor grinned. "With a crystal ball and someone wearing a mysterious cloak."

"That could be my aunt Anika," Jamal offered. "She's got loads of scarves."

They were laughing now, ideas tumbling over each other faster than Maya could write. Archery! A dunking booth! One of those machines where you try to grab toys with a claw! A magician! A puppet show! Face painting for dogs!

"Wait." Jamal held up his hand. "Face painting for dogs?"

"Why not?" Lily looked slightly offended. "Dogs have faces."

"Noted." Maya wrote it down, grinning.

Twenty minutes later, the list covered three pages. Maya sat back, shaking out her cramped hand.

"This is amazing," she said. "We've got enough ideas for the best fair Millbrook's ever seen."

"Better than the real one," Connor agreed. "We should do this every year."

"Councillor Davies won't know what hit him." Lily beamed at her sketch. She'd drawn the four of them standing beneath a banner reading MILLBROOK KIDS' FAIR, surrounded by bouncy castles and candy floss clouds and an improbably happy goat.

Only Jamal wasn't smiling.

He'd pulled out his phone again, tapping at the calculator like it was a particularly tricky maths problem.

"What?" Maya asked.

"I'm just..." He tapped a few more numbers. "Hang on."

Connor groaned. "Don't do the maths, mate. You'll ruin it."

"Someone has to do the maths." Jamal didn't look up. "Bouncy castle hire. For one day. Let me check."

He typed rapidly, eyes flicking across his screen. The others watched.

"Right." Jamal's voice had flattened. "So a decent bouncy castle, not the fancy one with turrets, just a normal one, costs about £80 to hire. For four hours."

Nobody spoke.

"That's nearly half our money," Lily said quietly. "Just for the bouncy castle."

"What about the petting zoo?" Maya asked, though she wasn't sure she wanted to know.

More tapping. "Mobile petting zoo with goats, rabbits, and guinea pigs. Minimum booking." Jamal swallowed. "£120."

"That's..." Connor was counting on his fingers. "That's more than half."

Jamal nodded.

The treehouse had gone very still.

"But we can't have a fair without a bouncy castle and a petting zoo," Lily said. "That's basically just a field with some tables."

"Look up candy floss machines," Connor said. "Maybe they're cheap."

They weren't. Hire cost: £65, plus ingredients. The hook-a-duck setup: £40 plus prizes. A coconut shy: £30 for the equipment, another £15 for coconuts. Hot dog cart: £90. Ice cream van: wouldn't come for less than a £200 booking.

"But that's our whole budget," Maya heard herself say. "Just for ice cream."

"The carousel with the painted horses," Jamal said, his voice strangely gentle. "I didn't even look it up. It doesn't matter. We couldn't afford one painted horse, let alone a whole carousel."

Maya stared at the list she'd written so enthusiastically. Three pages of brilliant ideas. Brilliant ideas that were fast becoming impossible to achieve.

"This isn't fair," Connor burst out. "£200 isn't enough. Why didn't they give us more? We can't do anything with £200."

"It's what we've got," Jamal said.

"IT'S NOT ENOUGH!"

"It's what we've got."

The calculator app glowed on Jamal's phone screen. £200. All those ideas. The numbers didn't lie.

Lily had stopped sketching.

"There must be a way," she said. "If we just... if we got creative... there must be something we can do."

"We can't magic money out of thin air," Connor said. "Trust me, I've tried."

"He's right." Maya surprised herself by speaking. The stones were back in her stomach, heavier than before. "We can't magic money out of thin air."

She looked down at the crumpled council notice, still sitting on the cable-reel table. "This is what Councillor Davies meant. This is what he knew we'd find out."

"That kids don't understand money?" Connor's voice was sharp.

"That wanting something really badly doesn't make it happen." Maya picked up the Official Crew Business notebook, flipping through the pages of dreams. "We want all of this. But look at it." She gestured at the three pages. "Three pages of ideas. And only £200 to spend."

Jamal stared at his calculator. "The maths doesn't work, does it?"

"Scarcity," Lily said quietly. She was looking at her drawing of the happy goat, which suddenly seemed a lot less happy.

"My dad says his patience is scarce," Connor offered, "but I think that might be a different thing."

"No he's right." Lily trailed off, frowning. "It's not just about money, is it?"

"Like... even if we had loads of money. The field's not that big. And we've only got eight weeks." She frowned at her sketchbook. "Everything's... not enough."

"Brilliant," Jamal muttered. "So we're stuck in three different ways."

Nobody argued with him.

Maya looked at the list again. Three pages of wonderful ideas. Three pages that might as well have been written in invisible ink, for all the good they'd do.

The bouncy castle alone would eat nearly half their money.

"So what do we do?" Lily asked. "Give up?"

The treehouse was quiet. Through the window, Maya could see the rooftops of Millbrook stretching toward the town centre, where the community hall stood empty of bunting, where no fair would be happening unless they succeeded.

"No," she said. "We don't give up. But we stop pretending we can have everything."

"And then what?" Connor asked.

"Then we figure out what we can have. What matters most." Maya tore the three pages of dreams from the notebook, setting them aside. She turned to a fresh page. "Councillor Davies thinks we'll fail because we're kids who don't understand that things cost money. Let's prove him wrong."

"By understanding?" Jamal's eyebrows rose. "That's your plan?"

"By choosing. Properly. Not just wishing for everything and hoping it works out." Maya wrote at the top of the clean page: MILLBROOK KIDS' FAIR - REAL PLAN. "We've got £200, eight weeks, one school field, and four of us. That's not nothing."

"It's not much," Connor pointed out.

"It's what we've got," Maya said, and this time the words sounded different. Not defeated, but clear and honest.

Lily picked up her sketchbook again. "So we have to choose. From all these ideas, we have to pick the ones we can actually do."

"The best ones," Jamal agreed. "The ones that will make the fair really work."

"But how do we know which ones are best?" Connor asked. "They all sound good. That's the problem."

Maya chewed her lip. The question hung in the treehouse, unanswered.

"I don't know," she admitted. "Not yet. But we've got to figure it out. If we just grab things randomly, we'll end up with half a bouncy castle and a goat with nowhere to stand."

"Could be worse," Jamal said. "Could end up with half a goat and a bouncy castle with nowhere to stand."

Despite everything, they laughed.

"Alright." Connor slapped his palms on the cable-reel table. "So we're doing this. We're planning a fair with two hundred quid and no idea how to choose what goes in it."

"That's the spirit," Maya said dryly.

"When you put it that way, it sounds mental."

"It is a bit mental," Lily agreed cheerfully. "But also exciting?"

Jamal was already making notes in his own neat handwriting. "We should meet again tomorrow. I'll research what things actually cost. Make a proper list with prices. Then at least we'll know what we're working with."

"I'll talk to my dad about the coconut shy," Connor said. "See what he can build for cheap."

"I'll ask my gran about the old fair," Maya added. "Maybe she remembers how it worked when it started. Before it got all big and expensive."

"And I'll sketch some layout options," Lily finished. "To check how much could actually fit on the school field."

They gathered their things: sketchbooks, phones, the remainder of the biscuit experiment. The afternoon had grown late without anyone noticing.

At the rope ladder, Connor paused. "Maya? Thanks, for not just... accepting it. When you saw that notice."

"Couldn't accept it," Maya said simply. "My gran's counting on seeing those painted horses."

"There won't be any painted horses, though. Not for two hundred quid."

"No." Maya thought of her grandmother's face when she talked about the old fair, the way her eyes lit up at memories fifty years old. "But we'll do our best to make it good. And that has to count for something, doesn't it?"

Connor nodded, then disappeared down the ladder. Lily followed, then Jamal, until Maya was alone in the treehouse with the crumpled council notice and a fresh page in her notebook that suddenly seemed full of possibility.

She looked at what she'd written. MILLBROOK KIDS' FAIR - REAL PLAN. Beneath it, nothing but empty space waiting to be filled.

Eight weeks. Four friends. £200.

It wasn't much. But as Maya climbed down from the treehouse, the first stars appearing in the darkening sky above Millbrook, she found herself smiling.

Councillor Davies thought kids didn't understand money. Maybe he was right, before today. But Maya understood something now that she hadn't understood this morning.

£200. All those ideas.

They'd have to pick. Somehow.

But they'd figure it out. They had to.

Chapter One Activities

Discussion Questions

1. The Millbrook Crew started with three pages of ideas for their fair. Have you ever wanted lots of things but couldn't have them all? What kinds of things were they?

2. When Maya saw the cancellation notice, she could have ignored it or complained about it. Instead, she went to the council meeting and then brought the challenge to her friends. Why do you think she made that choice?

3. Some of the crew didn't want Jamal to "do the maths" because they knew it would "ruin" their dreams. Was knowing the real costs helpful or unhelpful? Why might both things be true?

4. Lily realised that it wasn't just money that was limited. Time and space were limited too. Can you think of other things that might be "scarce" when planning something like a fair?

5. At the end of the chapter, Maya tears out the dream pages and starts fresh. Why was this an important moment? What do you think she'll write on the new page?

Quick Activities

Activity 1: My Wishlist Reality Check

Time: 10-15 minutes each

You'll need: Paper and pen

1. Write down 10 things you'd love to have or do (be as ambitious as you like!)
2. Next to each item, make a guess about what it might cost
3. Now imagine you have £20 to spend on these things
4. Circle which ones you could actually afford
5. How did it feel when you couldn't have everything on your list?

Activity 2: Scarcity Spotting

You'll need: Just your observation skills!

Over the next day, notice moments when you or people around you can't have everything they want. This might be:

- Not enough time to do all your homework AND play
- Not enough room in your bag for all your books
- Not enough money to buy everything at the shops
- Not enough space at the dinner table for everyone's elbows

Keep a mental tally. How many "scarcity moments" did you notice?

Activity 3: Fair Brainstorm

You'll need: Paper and coloured pens

Imagine YOU are planning a small fair at your school. You have £100 and one afternoon.

1. First, brainstorm every idea you can think of (like the Crew did, no limits!)
2. Then, put a star next to the ones you think might actually be possible
3. Finally, circle your top 3, the ones you'd definitely include

What made you choose those three?

Extended Activities

Extended Activity 1: The Scarcity Journal

Duration: One week

You'll need: A small notebook or paper stapled together

Create a "Scarcity Journal" for one week. Each day, write down:

- One moment when you had to choose because you couldn't have everything
- What you chose
- What you gave up
- How you felt about it

At the end of the week, look back at your entries. Do you notice any patterns? Were some choices harder than others? Why?

Extended Activity 2: Interview a Planner

Duration: 30-45 minutes

You'll need: An adult willing to be interviewed and paper

Find someone who has planned an event. For instance, this could be a birthday party, a school event, a work event, or a wedding. Ask them:

- What was your budget?
- What did you want to include but couldn't afford?
- How did you decide what to keep and what to cut?
- What advice would you give to someone planning their first event?

Write up what you learned. Were you surprised by anything they said?

Extended Activity 3: Design a Fair on a Budget

Duration: 1-2 hours (can be done in parts)

You'll need: Paper, ruler, coloured pencils, calculator

Design your own mini-fair on paper:

1. Create a simple map of your space
2. Set your budget: Choose an amount (try £150)
3. Research costs: Ask a grown-up to help you estimate what things might cost (or make reasonable guesses)
4. Plan your fair: Decide what to include and where things will go
5. Add up the cost: Does it fit your budget? If not, what will you change?
6. Present your plan: Explain to someone why you made the choices you did

Chapter 2 Parent/Educator Guide

Concept: Opportunity Cost

Every choice has a hidden price: the next-best alternative you didn't choose. This 'opportunity cost' is what you give up when you pick one option over another. The true cost of any decision includes not only what you spend, but what you sacrifice.

In a Child's World

Children face opportunity costs constantly, though they may not realise it. When they spend their birthday money on a toy, the opportunity cost is the book they could have bought instead.

In Your World

Adults navigate opportunity costs daily, often without naming them. Accepting a job promotion might mean less family time. Even small decisions carry hidden costs. The hour spent on emails is an hour not spent on the project you've been putting off. Recognising opportunity cost makes decisions clearer; you see the full picture of what you're choosing.

Why it Matters

Understanding opportunity cost transforms how children approach decisions. They learn to ask, "What am I giving up?" This deeper thinking helps them make choices they won't regret because they'll choose with full awareness. That's the beginning of wise decision-making.

2

Giving Up

The week that followed was the busiest of Maya's life.

On Monday, she spent her lunch break in the library with Jamal, researching hire costs for everything from tombola drums to portable generators. On Tuesday, she stayed late after school to meet with Mrs. Sharma about using the field. On Wednesday, she helped Connor raid his dad's garage for materials that might become a coconut shy. On Thursday, she and Lily walked the entire perimeter of the school field, measuring and re-measuring, trying to work out how much could actually fit.

By the weekend, Maya was so tired she nearly fell asleep in her cereal.

"You've got milk on your chin," her younger brother Oliver observed helpfully.

Maya wiped it away without looking up from her notebook, which was covered in scribbled calculations. The numbers still didn't add up. They never added up.

"Earth to Maya," her mum said as she passed. "You've been staring at that notebook for ten minutes."

"Just trying to work something out."

"The fair?" Her mum sat down opposite her, cradling her own cup of tea. "Dad said you were up late again last night."

"There's so much to figure out. We've got the budget sorted, sort of, and the space mapped out, sort of, but now we need volunteers, and we need to actually choose which activities to do, and we need..."

"To breathe, occasionally." Her mum reached over and gently closed the notebook. "The fair's not for another seven weeks. You don't have to solve everything at breakfast."

Maya wanted to argue, but her mum had that look. The one that meant arguing would be pointless and possibly result in confiscated notebooks.

"Speaking of things happening soon," her mum continued, in a tone that made Maya immediately suspicious, "have you checked the calendar lately?"

"Why?"

Her mum just sipped her tea.

Something cold crept up Maya's spine. She grabbed her phone and opened the calendar app, scrolling through the next few weeks. School. Fair planning. Homework. More fair planning. Football practice. Fair...

She stopped.

There it was. Saturday the 15th. Two weeks away.

REGIONAL FOOTBALL TRIALS - 9am-4pm - Westfield Sports Centre

"Oh no," Maya breathed.

"Oh yes," her mum said.

The regional trials. The ones Coach Peters had been preparing them for all season. The ones that happened once a year, that could get you onto the under-11s development squad, that could be the first step toward actually becoming a footballer! Maya had been dreaming about these trials since she was seven years old.

And they were scheduled for the same day as the fair committee's first big planning session. The one where they'd finalise all the activities.

"I can do both," Maya said immediately. "The trials are in the morning, I can get to the planning meeting in the afternoon."

"The trials run until four o'clock. The planning meeting starts at two." Her mum's voice was gentle but firm. "We've checked. There's no way to make both."

"But..."

"I know, love."

Maya stared at the calendar, willing the dates to rearrange themselves. They didn't.

"Can't the planning meeting be moved?"

"To when? Councillor Davies was very specific. He wants to see your plans before he'll approve the venue booking. That's the only available day to meet before the deadline."

"Can't the trials be moved?"

Her mum just looked at her.

"Right," Maya muttered. "Hundreds of kids. One venue. One date. Got it."

She pushed away from the table, suddenly not hungry anymore. The notebook sat there, closed, full of fair plans that suddenly seemed a lot less important than they had five minutes ago.

Or did they? That was the problem. They didn't seem less important. They seemed exactly as important. Which meant she had two extremely important things happening at exactly the same time, and she could only be in one place.

"I don't know what to do," she admitted.

Her mum reached across the table and squeezed her hand. "I know, love. I know."

. . . .

The treehouse felt different that afternoon.

Usually, Saturday meetings were relaxed. Biscuits and rambling conversations and Connor's increasingly elaborate theories about which teachers were secretly robots. But today, everyone had brought something heavy with them, and Maya didn't just mean Jamal's overstuffed folder of research.

"So," Jamal said, once they'd settled into their usual spots. "I've done the costings."

He spread out a series of printed pages on the cable-reel table. Numbers marched across them in neat columns: activity names, hire costs, space requirements, volunteer needs.

"This is everything we could realistically afford," he continued, "based on the £200 and the space Lily measured." He pointed to a shorter list at the bottom of one page. "And this is what would actually fit on the field if we include pathways and a first aid area and somewhere for people to queue."

Connor leaned over to look. "That's... not much."

"No," Jamal agreed. "It's not."

The list read:

Affordable and fits on field:

- Coconut shy (if Connor's dad builds it) - £15
- Cake stall (donated cakes) - £0
- Face painting (Lily) - £12
- Tombola - £30
- Hook-a-duck (small version) - £25
- Guess the weight of the cake - £0
- Splat-the-rat (if we make it ourselves) - £8

"That's seven things," Lily said. "Seven things doesn't sound like a fair. That sounds like a... a slightly busy afternoon."

"We could add more if we skip some of these," Jamal said carefully. "Like, if we don't do the tombola, we could afford a small bouncy castle instead. But then we'd have fewer activities overall, just one big one and a few small ones."

"What about the hook-a-duck AND the bouncy castle?" Connor asked.

"Then we can't afford prizes for either of them. And we'd have to cut the face painting supplies."

"So Lily couldn't do face painting?"

"Not unless someone donates the paints."

Lily's face fell. She'd been practising designs all week. Maya had seen the tigers and butterflies and superheroes filling page after page of her sketchbook.

"This is impossible," Connor said flatly. "Every time we try to add something good, we have to take away something else good."

"That's sort of the point." Maya hadn't meant to speak, but the words came out anyway. "That's what we figured out last week, isn't it? Scarcity. We can't have everything."

"I know we can't have everything, but I thought we could have... more than seven things."

"We can," Jamal said. "If we're willing to give things up."

The phrase hung in the air, and Maya felt it land differently than it might have yesterday. Give things up. She thought about the football trials, about the calendar notification glowing on her phone, and about the choice she couldn't seem to make.

"Erm, guys? This reminds me..." she heard herself say.

Everyone looked at her.

"Of what?" Lily asked.

Maya pulled out her phone, showing them the calendar. "The regional trials. They're the same day as our final planning meeting."

"Can't you do both?" Connor asked.

"No. I checked. It's one or the other."

Silence fell over the treehouse.

"Oh, Maya." Lily's voice was soft. "You've been training for those trials all year."

"I know."

"But the fair..."

"I know."

Jamal was frowning at his folder, not meeting anyone's eyes. After a moment, he pulled out another piece of paper, this one handwritten.

"I've got something too," he said quietly. "Something I've been thinking about."

They waited.

"I've been saving for a new bike. For ages. Nearly two years." He stared at the paper. "I've got £73. I was going to ask my parents to match it for my birthday next month, and then I'd finally have enough."

"The blue one?" Connor asked. "The one you showed us?"

"Yeah." Jamal swallowed. "But I was thinking... if I put my savings into the fair fund, we'd have so much more to work with."

"Jamal, you can't…" Lily started.

"I can. It's my money. I can do what I want with it."

"But you've been saving forever!"

"I know." His voice cracked slightly. "That's why it's hard."

Maya stared at her friend Jamal, who'd had a picture of that blue bike on his bedroom wall for the last year. He'd give that up? For the fair?

"You don't have to," she said.

"I know I don't have to. But if I did... we could do so much more. We could actually make something good instead of something... alright."

"Alright is not so bad," Connor offered weakly.

"Alright doesn't save the Millbrook Fair," Jamal replied. "Alright doesn't prove Councillor Davies wrong."

Another silence stretched between them. Outside, a bird chirped. An ordinary sound that seemed to highlight how unusual the silence was.

"I don't know if I can give up the trials," Maya admitted. "I want to help with the fair, I really do, but football... It's who I am. When I'm playing, I feel like..."

She struggled for words. "Like everything makes sense."

"So don't give it up," Connor said. "Go to the trials. We'll figure out the meeting."

"But if I'm not there, Councillor Davies will think…"

"We'll handle Councillor Davies."

"Will we, though?"

Nobody answered.

Lily had been quiet for a while, which usually meant she was thinking something important. Now she spoke, her voice careful.

"It's just..." Lily paused, frowning at her sketchbook. "Whichever one Maya picks, something good disappears. That's the horrible bit."

Lily pulled her sketchbook onto her lap, flipping to a fresh page. She started drawing. Two paths splitting from a single point. "When Maya goes to the trials, she gets football. But she also... loses the meeting. And if she goes to the meeting instead..."

"I lose football," Maya finished quietly.

"Either way, something's gone." Lily added small drawings at the end of each path. A football on one, a clipboard on the other.

"My bike," Jamal said slowly. "If I put the money in the fair fund..." He stared at his hands. "The bike's gone. Whatever we spend it on."

Connor was thinking. "So it's not just about what things cost in money. It's about what else you could've done instead."

"Yeah." Lily looked at her drawing. "The path you didn't take."

Maya thought about the calendar again. Football trials. Planning meeting. Two things she wanted badly, and only time and energy for one.

"I keep thinking I'm choosing football," she said slowly. "But I'm also choosing to miss the meeting. It's the same choice, somehow. Just... backwards."

Jamal nodded slowly, like something was clicking into place.

"Well that's depressing," Connor announced.

"It's not depressing. It's just... true, I guess." Lily added. "And once you see it that way, you can't unsee it."

They took a break after that. Biscuits and a half-hearted attempt at normal conversation. But Maya's mind kept circling back to the same question: trials or meeting? Football or fair?

What made it worse was that she couldn't even say which one she wanted more. She wanted both. She wanted both exactly equally, which meant there was no obvious answer, no clear winner.

"Let's go see my dad," Connor said suddenly.

Everyone looked at him.

"About the coconut shy," he explained. "He said he'd help, remember? Maybe actually doing something will help us stop thinking in circles."

It wasn't a bad idea. At least it would get them out of the treehouse, away from Jamal's spreadsheets and Lily's forking-path drawings and the uncomfortable questions that seemed to hang in every corner.

. . . .

Connor's dad was in the garage, surrounded by planks of wood and the smell of sawdust. He looked up as the four of them trooped through the side door, pushing his safety goggles up onto his forehead.

"The Millbrook Crew! Come to help with the shy, have you?"

"Something like that," Connor said. "Dad, can I ask you something?"

"You can ask me anything. Doesn't mean I'll have a sensible answer."

"When you ran your stall at the fair last year, the one with the wooden puzzles, how did you decide what to sell?"

Mr. Murphy set down his sandpaper, considering the question with unexpected seriousness.

"Well, that's a good question. I wanted to sell all sorts: puzzles, birdhouses, those little wooden cars like I made for you when you were small. I had plans for a whole catalogue, I did. But then I sat down and worked out how many hours I had, and how long each thing took to make, and how much space I had on the stall..."

"And?"

"And I realised I could do puzzles well, or I could do everything badly." He smiled, with a slight sense of regret. "First year I tried the fair, I brought all sorts. Bit of this, bit of that. None of it was my best work, because I'd spread myself too thin. Sold barely anything. People could tell I'd rushed."

"So you just did puzzles the next year?" Lily asked.

"Just puzzles. Took me ages to decide, mind. Giving up the birdhouses felt like giving up a piece of myself, if that makes sense. I'd been making birdhouses since before Connor was born."

Maya thought about football. About how playing made her feel like herself.

"But you couldn't do both properly," she said quietly. "Not with the time you had."

"Not with the time I had," Mr. Murphy agreed. "And once I stopped trying to do everything, the puzzles that year were the best I'd ever made."

"Did people buy them?" Jamal asked.

"Sold out by lunchtime. Had people asking if I'd take orders for Christmas." Mr. Murphy grinned. "Sometimes giving something up is how you make space for something to succeed."

The crew exchanged glances. It wasn't quite advice. Mr. Murphy hadn't told them what to do, but it was useful. A different way of looking at the problem.

"Now," Connor's dad said, picking up his sandpaper again, "who wants to help me turn these planks into something people can throw balls at?"

They worked until the light faded. Measuring, sawing (Mr. Murphy did the actual sawing; the crew did the holding and fetching), sanding rough edges until the wood was smooth. By the end of it, the basic frame of a coconut shy stood in the garage, unpainted but solid.

"We actually made something," Lily said, running her hand along the wooden edge

"First thing for the fair," Connor agreed, grinning. "See? We're not totally useless."

But Maya was quiet, thinking about what Mr. Murphy had said. About giving things up and making space for other things to succeed.

She thought about her grandmother, who'd been asking about the fair every time Maya saw her. Will there be the coconut shy? I do love the coconut shy. Your grandfather won me a goldfish at the coconut shy, you know. We had that fish for seven years...

She thought about Coach Peters, who'd told her last week that she had real potential. The trials are your chance to show what you can do, Maya. Don't let it slip.

She thought about Councillor Davies' sceptical face at the council meeting, about the way he'd laughed when Mrs. Sharma suggested children could make good choices.

All of those choices still needed to be made.

That night, Maya sat on her bed with her phone in her hand.

The calendar glowed: REGIONAL FOOTBALL TRIALS. And beneath it: FAIR COMMITTEE MEETING.

She couldn't have both. She'd been pretending she could, somehow, if she just thought hard enough. But Lily's drawing kept appearing in her mind. Two paths, one person, no way to walk both at once.

She opened a new message to the Millbrook Crew group chat.

I've been thinking, she typed.

Then stopped. Stared at the blinking cursor.

I've been thinking about what Connor's dad said. About how giving up the birdhouses let him make the puzzles really good.

Send.

Three dots appeared immediately. Jamal was typing.

Me too. Still thinking about the bike.

Lily joined: *I keep drawing the two paths. Over and over.*

Connor: *My dad asked if we were okay. Said we looked like we were carrying something heavy.*

Maya smiled to herself. Trust Connor's dad to notice.

She typed again: *I'm going to the meeting. Not the trials.*

The words sat on her screen for a long moment before she pressed send. When she did, her heart

hammered, but something else settled, something that felt almost like relief.

The responses came quickly:

Jamal: *Are you sure?*

Maya: *No. But I'm choosing anyway. The fair needs me there. Coach Peters will understand. There'll be other trials.*

Lily: *There'll be other trials.*

Connor: *You're braver than me. I'd choose football.*

Maya: *You'd choose whatever you thought was right. We all would.*

She set down her phone and lay back on her bed, staring at the ceiling. The trials. Gone. Just like that. A door closing. A path not taken.

It hurt. More than she'd expected.

But maybe that was okay. Maybe it was supposed to hurt when you make difficult decisions.

Her phone buzzed one more time. Jamal.

I'm keeping my bike savings. For now. But I'll help find other ways to raise money. We'll make this work, Maya. Together.

Maya smiled in the darkness.

Together, she typed back.

And then, because she couldn't help herself: *Now go to sleep. We've got a fair to plan.*

Chapter Two Activities

Discussion Questions

1. Maya discovered that the football trials and the fair planning meeting were on the same day. Have you ever wanted to do two things at once but couldn't? What did you choose, and how did it feel to miss the other thing?

2. Jamal thought about putting his bike savings into the fair fund. Why do you think he decided to keep his savings in the end? Was that the right choice?

3. Mr. Murphy said that giving up the birdhouses let him make his puzzles "the best he'd ever made." Can you think of a time when focusing on one thing helped you do it better?

4. Lily drew two paths splitting from one point to help Maya think about her choice. Why do you think seeing it as a picture helped? Do you prefer to think in words or pictures?

5. Maya said choosing the meeting over football "hurt." Do you think all important choices hurt a little bit? Or can some be easy?

Quick Activities

Activity 1: The Two-Path Drawing

Time: 10 minutes

You'll need: Paper and pencil

1. Think of a choice you're facing right now. It could be small (what to do after school) or bigger (which club to join).
2. Draw a single dot in the middle of a piece of paper. This is you, right now.
3. Draw two paths leading away from the dot in different directions.
4. At the end of each path, draw or write what you'd get if you chose that option.
5. Now add one more thing: on each path, write what you'd MISS if you went the other way.

Does seeing it drawn out change how you think about the choice?

Activity 2: The Hidden Cost Spotter

Time: 5–10 minutes

Every choice has a hidden cost. Maya's hidden cost for going to the meeting was missing the football trials.

For each choice below, spot the hidden cost:

- You spend your birthday money on a video game.
- You stay up late reading a brilliant book.
- You join the drama club instead of the football team.
- You eat the last biscuit.

Challenge: Can you think of a choice where the hidden cost is really, really small?

Activity 3: The 'What If' Game

Time: 10 minutes

Imagine Maya went to the football trials instead of the fair meeting:

- What might have happened at the trials?
- What might have happened at the fair meeting without Maya?
- How might Maya have felt afterwards?
- Would the fair still have happened? Would it have been different?

Now try it with your own choice:

Think of a choice you made recently. What if you'd chosen the other option? Play out the 'What If' in your head. Does it change how you feel about your actual choice?

Extended Activities

Extended Activity 1: The Trade-Off Journal

Time: 5 minutes each day for one week

1. Get a small notebook or use a notes app on a phone or tablet.
2. Each day, write down ONE choice you made. It can be tiny ("I had toast instead of cereal") or bigger ("I went to Emma's house instead of practising piano").
3. Next to your choice, write what you gave up (the hidden cost)
4. At the end of the week, look back. Which choices were easy? Which were hard? Did any surprise you?

Extended Activity 2: Interview a Grown-Up

Time: 20–30 minutes

1. Ask a parent, grandparent, teacher, or other adult if you can interview them about choices.
2. Ask them these questions (and any others you think of):
   - "What's one big choice you had to make where you couldn't have both things?"
   - "What did you choose, and what did you give up?"
   - "How did you decide?"
   - "Do you ever wonder what would have happened if you'd chosen differently?"
   - "Is there anything you gave up that helped you do something else really well?"
3. Write down or draw what you learned. Were you surprised by any of their answers?

Extended Activity 3: The Time Budget

Time: 30 minutes to set up, then ongoing

Time is one of the most important things we have to budget, and unlike money, you can't save it up!

1. Pick one day next week (a school day works well).
2. List everything you HAVE to do that day (school, meals, sleep, homework, etc.) and how long each takes.
3. Add up the hours. How much "free" time is left?
4. Now list everything you WANT to do (play games, read, see friends, watch TV, practise a hobby).
5. Can you fit it all in? If not, what will you choose, and what will you give up?
6. After the day, look back. Did you stick to your "time budget"? What would you change?

Chapter 3 Parent/Educator Guide

Concept: Cost-Benefit Analysis

Cost-benefit analysis is a way to compare options by listing the good points and bad points of each, then weighing them against each other. The process reveals trade-offs and can surface hidden assumptions about what you value most.

In a Child's World

Children make comparisons constantly, though usually informally: "The swimming party is exciting but my best friends are going bowling." In this chapter, children will see that this structured thinking doesn't eliminate difficult feelings, but it does make the reasoning visible and shareable.

In Your World

You likely use cost-benefit thinking for major decisions: comparing job offers, evaluating whether to renovate or move, weighing holiday options. Businesses and governments formalise this process extensively. As adults know, the numbers sometimes point one way while your instincts point another.

Why it Matters

Learning to systematically compare options is a life skill that transfers everywhere: evaluating university courses, making career decisions, and countless daily choices. More importantly, the process of working through benefits and costs moves from vague feelings to clear reasons.

3

Weighing It Up

Six weeks until the fair.

The Millbrook Crew sat in their usual circle in the treehouse, but nothing else felt usual. Jamal's research folder had grown to three times its original size. Lily's sketchbook was filled with layout options. Twelve different arrangements of the school field, each one crossed out and revised. Connor had sawdust embedded in his jumper from daily trips to his dad's garage. And Maya had dark circles under her eyes that even her mum's makeup wouldn't be able to hide.

They had information, options, and a growing sense that they were going in circles.

"Right," Maya said, pulling the Official Crew Business notebook onto her lap. "Let's make the final decisions. Today. No more putting it off."

"Agreed," said Connor. "My dad keeps asking what colours to paint the coconut shy. I can't tell him if I don't know what else we're having."

"Okay." Maya flipped to a fresh page. "So our definite activities are the coconut shy, because it's already built, and the cake stall, because it's free. That leaves us with..." She checked Jamal's cost sheet. "£185 for everything else."

"Face painting," Lily said immediately. "We have to have face painting."

"Tombola," Connor countered. "Everyone loves a tombola. You get prizes."

"Hook-a-duck," Jamal suggested. "It's classic. And it doesn't need electricity, which saves money on the generator."

"What about the bouncy castle?" Lily asked. "If we got a small one..."

"Small ones are still £80," Jamal said. "That's nearly half our remaining budget."

"But it's a bouncy castle! Kids love bouncy castles!"

"Kids also love face painting. And tombolas. And hook-a-duck."

"So we do all of them?"

"We can't afford all of them. Face painting is £12, tombola is £30, hook-a-duck is £25. That's £67, which leaves us £118. The bouncy castle is £80, which leaves £38. That's not enough for..."

"What about splat-the-rat?" Connor interrupted. "We said we'd make that ourselves. £8 for materials."

"Fine, add splat-the-rat. That's £75 in total without the bouncy castle, leaving £110. With the bouncy castle it's £155, leaving £30."

"£30 isn't enough for anything else useful."

"Exactly my point."

Maya's pen had stopped moving. She stared at the notebook page, which had become a mess of numbers and crossing-out and question marks.

"This isn't working," she said.

"What isn't working?" Connor asked.

"This. Just... shouting out things we want and hoping the numbers magically fit." She rubbed her forehead. "We've had this same conversation three times now. We always end up stuck in the same place."

"Because the maths doesn't work," Jamal said quietly.

"No, because we keep arguing about which things are better, and we never actually figure out how to compare them." Maya set down her pen. "Lily thinks face painting is essential. Connor thinks tombola is essential. I think..." She trailed off. "I don't even know what I think anymore."

The only sound was the wind in the oak leaves outside.

"I have an idea," Jamal said.

Everyone looked at him.

"You're not going to like it."

"Tell us anyway," Maya said.

Jamal reached into his folder and pulled out a fresh

sheet of paper, blank, with faint grid lines. "We make a list. A proper one. With columns."

Connor groaned. "Jamal, mate, we've got lists. We've got lists of lists. We've got so many lists I'm seeing grid lines in my sleep."

"Not that kind of list." Jamal was already drawing lines, dividing the page into sections. "A comparison list. Where we write down the good points and the bad points about each option, and then actually look at them side by side."

"That sounds..." Lily hesitated. "A bit complicated?"

"It sounds boring," Connor said flatly. "Sorry, but it does."

"Maybe boring is what we need." Maya leaned forward, watching Jamal's pen move. "What have you got?"

Jamal held up the paper. He'd created a simple grid:

Activity	Good Points	Bad Points	Cost
Bouncy castle			£80
Face painting			£12
Tombola			£30
Hook-a-duck			£25
Splat-the-rat			£8

"We fill it in together," Jamal explained. "All the good points about each option, why we'd want it. And all the bad points, why we might not. Then we can actually see what we're comparing."

"Instead of just arguing," Maya said slowly.

"Instead of just arguing."

Connor looked sceptical, but Lily was already reaching for her coloured pencils. "Can I do the writing? I'll make it pretty."

"It doesn't need to be pretty..."

"Everything needs to be pretty. It helps me think."

Jamal surrendered the paper. Within minutes, Lily had transformed his grid into something that looked almost like a work of art. Headers in different colours, little icons next to each activity, decorative borders that somehow made the whole task feel less like homework.

"Right," Maya said. "Bouncy castle. Good points."

"Kids love it," Connor said immediately.

"It's exciting," Lily added. "It's the first thing people notice."

"It keeps children entertained for ages," Maya contributed. "Parents can relax."

"It's impressive," Jamal admitted. "It makes the fair look professional. Like a real event."

Lily wrote furiously, her neat handwriting filling the "Good Points" column.

"Bad points?" Maya prompted.

"It's expensive," Jamal said. "£80. That's over 40% of our remaining budget."

"It takes up loads of space," Connor added. "We measured, remember? A proper bouncy castle needs, like, a quarter of the field just for safety zones."

"It needs supervision," Maya said. "Someone has to watch it the whole time. Make sure kids aren't bouncing into each other."

"It needs electricity," Jamal finished. "Which means we need a generator, which we haven't budgeted for."

Lily's pen moved more slowly now. The "Bad Points" column was growing.

"Okay." Maya felt something shifting, some new clarity emerging. "Let's move onto face painting."

"Good points: it's cheap," Jamal started.

"It's creative," Lily said, brightening. "Kids get to choose their designs. They take something home with them, well, on their face."

"It doesn't take much space," Connor added. "Just a table and chair."

"Parents take photos," Maya said. "They share them. It's good for, you know, showing people the fair was fun."

"I can do it," Lily added quietly. "So we don't need to hire anyone."

They moved to the bad points.

"It's slow," Jamal said. "One face at a time. Creates queues."

"If Lily's doing it, she can't help with other things," Maya realised. "She's stuck at the face painting station all day."

"Some kids are wiggly," Connor said. "My little cousin had to have his tiger redone three times because he wouldn't sit still."

"And it depends on Lily," Jamal added carefully. "If she's ill, or needs a break, we don't have backup."

Lily's pen hesitated over that last point, but she wrote it down anyway.

They continued through the list. Tombola, hook-a-duck, splat-the-rat, filling in good points and bad points for each. By the time they finished, the grid covered two full pages of Lily's sketchbook, a rainbow of observations and considerations.

"Now what?" Connor asked.

Maya stared at the pages. "Now we... compare?"

"But how?" Lily asked. "Face painting has lots of good things, but so does the bouncy castle. They're different kinds of good."

"That's the problem," Jamal said. "An apple and an orange are both fruit, but you can't say one is more fruit than the other."

"You could say one is more delicious," Connor offered.

"But that's opinion. Different people like different things."

"So we're stuck again?"

Jamal shook his head slowly. "Not necessarily. What if we scored them?"

. . . .

The scoring idea took some explaining.

"We give each activity a score," Jamal said, sketching on a fresh piece of paper. "Like, for how important each good point is, and how bad each bad point is."

"Scores out of what?" Maya asked.

"I don't know. Ten?"

"Why ten?"

"Because ten is easy. And it's what Mr. Patel uses for maths quizzes."

Connor snorted. "This is nothing like Mr. Patel's maths quizzes."

"It's exactly like our maths quizzes. We're weighing things up. Seeing what adds up to more."

"Benefits," Maya said suddenly.

Everyone looked at her.

"Mrs. Sharma said something about this once. In assembly." Maya was trying to remember. "About how the school decides things. She said they write down the benefits, the good stuff, and the costs, the bad stuff. And then they compare them. My mum complains about it at work. They have to do reports. With numbers and everything."

"Brilliant," Connor muttered. "We're doing homework. Homework we've given ourselves. In our treehouse. On a Saturday."

"Do you want to keep arguing forever?" Maya asked.

Connor slumped. "Fine. Let's do the weird scoring thing."

They started with the bouncy castle, going through each benefit and each cost, assigning points based on how much it mattered. The conversations were intense.

"'Kids love it' is worth at least nine points," Lily insisted.

"But 'it costs £80' is worth negative eight points," Jamal countered.

"You can't just cancel them out!"

"Why not? That's literally what we're doing."

"Because loving something and it being expensive aren't the same kind of thing."

"Then what kind of things are they?"

They argued about everything. Was "kids love it" worth more than "it costs £80"? Was looking impressive worth the space it took up? Was Lily being stuck at face painting worse than someone having to watch the bouncy castle all day?

After an hour, they had scores:

Activity	Benefits Score	Costs Score	Difference
Bouncy castle	32	36	-4
Face painting	27	19	+8
Tombola	24	12	+12
Hook-a-duck	26	14	+12
Splat-the-rat	18	8	+10

"So tombola and hook-a-duck are tied for best," Connor said, squinting at the numbers. "Then splat-the-rat, then face painting, then bouncy castle."

"That can't be right," Lily protested. "The bouncy castle is the most exciting thing. How is it last?"

"Because it costs loads and needs loads of space and needs electricity and needs supervision," Jamal said. "All those bad things add up."

"But the good things..."

"Also add up. They just don't cancel out the bad things."

Lily crossed her arms, looking genuinely upset. "This doesn't feel right. Numbers can't tell you what's most important."

"The numbers aren't deciding for us," Maya said slowly. "We decided when we picked the scores. The numbers just... showed us what we'd already thought. Sort of."

"Then what's the point?"

"The point is we can see it all at once. Instead of everyone arguing about their favourite thing, we can look at..." Maya gestured at the table. "Look at all of it together. The whole picture."

"But we still don't agree," Lily said. "I think the bouncy castle should score higher. Connor thinks the tombola is too high because he doesn't like tombolas..."

"I never said I don't like tombolas!"

"You said they were 'basically just a fancy raffle.'"

"That's not the same as not liking them!"

"Okay, stop." Maya held up her hands. "Lily's right. The scores are different depending on who's doing the scoring. If I'd given points, the bouncy castle might be higher. If Connor had done it..."

"The bouncy castle would definitely be higher," Connor confirmed. "I love bouncy castles."

"So the analysis doesn't actually work?" Jamal looked disheartened.

"No, it does work. It's just not..." Maya struggled for words. "It's not magic. It doesn't make the decision for us. It just helps us see what we're deciding."

For a moment, nobody argued. Outside, a squirrel ran along a branch, chittering at something only it could see.

"My mum says something like this about dinner," Lily said eventually. "She asks what everyone wants, but then she still has to pick. Knowing what people want doesn't actually cook anything."

"So we've considered everything," Connor said. "Now what?"

Maya looked at the numbers again. At the good points and bad points laid out so carefully. At the scores that reflected their best attempts to be fair and thorough.

"Now we choose," she said. "But we choose knowing

what we're choosing. Knowing what we're getting and what we're giving up."

"Without the bouncy castle." The words felt heavier than Maya expected. "It's just too expensive for what we get. The money and space could give us three or four other things."

"But it's so impressive."

"So is a fair that actually works." Maya reached over and squeezed Lily's hand. "It's not that it's bad. It's just... not right for us. Not this time."

Jamal looked at the chart, then at Maya. His face had changed. Not smiling exactly, but something close to it.

"We actually figured it out," he said quietly. "Not just argued until someone gave up. We actually... figured it out."

The final decisions came faster after that.

With the bouncy castle off the table, they had £185 to work with. They chose:

- **Face painting (£12):** Lily's talent was too good to waste, and kids genuinely loved going home with painted faces.
- **Tombola (£30):** Everyone loved winning prizes, and it was easy to run.
- **Hook-a-duck (£25):** A classic. Didn't need electricity. Worked for all ages.
- **Splat-the-rat (£8):** Cheap, funny, and they could build it themselves.
- **Welly wanging (£5):** Connor found an old set of wellies in his garage. Basically free hilarity.
- **Guess the sweeties in a jar (£6):** Everyone had a jar, and sweets were cheap.

Total: £86 for activities, leaving £99 for prizes, supplies, signs, and emergencies.

"We have nearly £100 left," Lily said, surprised. "I thought we'd spend everything."

"We need contingency," Jamal said. "That's what my dad calls it. Money for things that go wrong."

"What could go wrong?"

"I don't know. That's why it's contingency. For the things you don't expect."

Maya wrote the final list in the Official Crew Business notebook, her handwriting more careful than usual. This was real now. These were the actual activities for the fair. Not dreams anymore.

"We should tell Councillor Davies," she said. "Show him we've made proper choices. With reasons."

"We should show him the whole analysis," Jamal agreed, straightening his research folder with pride. "All the options we considered, and why we picked the ones we did."

"He'll probably say it's not as good as a bouncy castle," Connor said.

"Maybe. But he can't say we didn't think it through."

"And it is good," Lily said, her enthusiasm returning. "Face painting and tombola and hook-a-duck and splat-the-rat and welly wanging and the sweetie jar thing. That's six activities! Plus the coconut shy and cake stall makes eight. Eight things! That's a proper fair."

"A proper fair that we planned properly," Maya added. "No grabbing random things. No hoping for the best."

She looked around at her friends. At Jamal's colour-coded folder, at Lily's beautiful charts, at Connor who was already sketching splat-the-rat designs on a napkin.

"I was wrong," Connor announced.

Everyone stared at him.

"About the lists being boring. They weren't boring. They were just..." He searched for the word. "Useful, I guess. Annoyingly useful."

"That's the nicest thing you've ever said about maths," Jamal said.

"Don't get used to it." But Connor was smiling.

. . . .

That evening, Maya spread everything out on the kitchen table, the lists, the scores, the final decisions, and showed her mum.

"Cost-benefit analysis," her mum said, sounding impressed. "Did you learn that at school?"

"We kind of figured it out. By accident."

Her mum picked up Lily's colourful chart, examining the careful columns of benefits and costs. "This is what I do at work, actually. When we have to decide between projects."

"We just wanted to stop arguing," Maya admitted.

"That's usually why people start analysing things properly. Because arguing is exhausting." Her mum set down the chart. "What did you decide?"

Maya explained the final list, the six activities they'd chosen, the £99 contingency, and the reasons behind each decision.

"No bouncy castle?" Her mum raised an eyebrow.

"Costs outweighed the benefits."

"Even though you love bouncy castles?"

"Even though I love bouncy castles." The words surprised her, but they were true. "It wasn't just about what I wanted. The fair needed other things more."

Her mum was quiet for a moment. Then she pulled Maya into a hug, unexpected and fierce and smelling of the lavender perfume she always wore.

"I'm proud of you," she said into Maya's hair. "This is hard stuff. A lot of grown-ups never learn to think this way."

"It didn't make choosing easier," Maya said. "We still had to choose."

"No. It never makes choosing easier. But it makes choosing better." Her mum pulled back, holding Maya's shoulders. "There's a difference between a hard choice and a blind one. You're not choosing blindly anymore."

Maya thought about that as she helped clear the table, stacking the carefully-created charts into a neat pile.

Not choosing blindly.

That was something, wasn't it? Even if the choices were still hard. Even if giving up the bouncy castle still stung a little. At least they'd made those choices with reasons and understanding.

The benefits and the costs. All weighed up. All considered.

Maya smiled and reached for the dishcloth. Six weeks until the fair. And for the first time, she actually believed they might pull it off.

Chapter Three Activities

Discussion Questions

1. Connor said making lists was "boring" at first, but later admitted they were "annoyingly useful." Have you ever found something boring that turned out to be helpful? What was it?

2. Lily got upset when the bouncy castle scored lowest, even though she'd helped create the scoring system. Why do you think it felt wrong to her, even though the numbers made sense?

3. Maya realised that "the numbers aren't deciding for us... We decided when we picked the scores". What do you think she meant by that?

4. The Crew gave up the bouncy castle even though everyone wanted one. Is it always right to pick what the analysis says, or are there times when you should ignore it?

5. Maya's mum said there's a difference between "a hard choice and a blind one." What do you think she meant? Can you give an example of each?

Quick Activities

Activity 1: The Good Points/Bad Points Grid

Time: 10-15 minutes

1. Think of something you need to decide. Maybe: which book to read next, what to ask for as a gift, or how to spend a free afternoon.
2. Draw a grid with three columns: OPTION, GOOD POINTS, BAD POINTS
3. List 2–3 options in the first column.
4. For each option, write ALL the good things about it. Then ALL the bad things.
5. Look at your completed grid. Does one option stand out? Or is it still hard to choose?

Remember: The grid helps you see clearly, but YOU still make the choice!

Activity 2: The Scoring Game

Time: 10 minutes

Scenario: You're choosing a pet.

Your options are: A dog, a cat, or a goldfish.

Score each of these factors from 1–10 for EACH pet:

- How fun to play with?
- How much work to look after? (Lower score = more work)
- How cuddly?
- How expensive? (Lower score = more expensive)

Add up the scores. Which pet 'wins'?

Now ask yourself: Did you agree with the numbers? If not, why not?

Activity 3: Change the Scores

Time: 10 minutes

1. Go back to your pet scores from Quick Activity 2.
2. Now imagine you're someone who REALLY values cuddliness. Double your "cuddly" scores for each pet.
3. Add up the new totals. Did the winner change?
4. Try it again, but now imagine you're someone who doesn't have much money. Double the "expensive" scores.

What did you learn? The "best" choice depends on what matters most to the person choosing!

Extended Activities

Extended Activity 1: Family Decision Night

Time: 30 minutes with your family

1. Choose a decision your family needs to make together. Ideas: where to go for a day out, what to have for a special dinner, or how to redecorate a room.
2. Make a Good Points / Bad Points grid together, with everyone contributing ideas.
3. Try scoring the options. Does everyone give the same scores? (They probably won't!)
4. Discuss: How do you decide when people disagree about what's important?
5. Make the final choice together. Did the grid help, even if you didn't just pick the "highest scorer"?

Reflection questions:

- *Was the final decision different from what you'd have chosen without the grid?*
- *Did anyone feel like the numbers said one thing but their heart said another?*

Extended Activity 2: The School Lunch Comparison

Time: 20 minutes

3. Think about your options for lunch on a school day (school dinner, packed lunch from home, buying something from a shop, etc.).
4. Create a Good Points / Bad Points grid for each option. Think about: taste, healthiness, cost, etc.
5. Score each factor. Add up the totals.
6. Which option "wins" according to your analysis?
7. Over the next week, pay attention to which option you actually choose each day. Does your real choice match your analysis? If not, why not?

Sometimes we discover that what we SAY matters isn't the same as what actually influences our choices!

Extended Activity 3: Design Your Dream Bedroom

Time: 45 minutes to 1 hour

1. Your budget is £500. That has to cover EVERYTHING: furniture, decorations, paint, bedding, posters, storage...
2. First, make a wish list of everything you'd want.
3. Research rough prices online or ask an adult to help estimate. Add up your wish list total.
4. Now create a Good Points/Bad Points grid for your top 10 items. Consider: How much do I want it? How useful is it? How much does it cost?
5. Use your analysis to make your final choices. Can you get the most important things within £500?
6. Draw or describe your final bedroom design. What did you have to give up? Are you happy with your choices?

Chapter 4 Parent/Educator Guide

Concept: Incentives

Incentives are the rewards and consequences that influence people's choices. They can be tangible or intangible. Different people respond to different incentives, and sometimes offering the wrong incentive can backfire, undermining the behaviour you're trying to encourage.

In a Child's World

Children encounter incentives through house points at school, pocket money for chores, and praise for good behaviour. They also experience the limits of incentives. This chapter helps children to recognise this complexity.

In Your World

Adults see incentives through workplace bonuses, loyalty schemes, etc. Incentives often have unintended consequences. Paying people for blood donations can reduce donations. Effective approaches often combine incentives to appeal to different motivations.

Why it Matters

Understanding incentives helps children to recognise when others are trying to influence their behaviour. Advertising and peer pressure work through incentives. Second, it helps them motivate others more effectively, whether organising a group project or simply asking for help.

4

Worth Their While

Four weeks until the fair.

The sign-up sheet had been on the school notice board for five days.

The lines were still blank.

"Maybe people haven't seen it," Lily suggested, though she didn't sound convinced.

"It's next to the lunch menu," Connor pointed out. "Everyone sees the lunch menu."

"Maybe they've seen it but they're thinking about it."

"For five days?"

The four of them stood in front of the notice board, staring at their lonely sign-up sheet as streams of students flowed past on their way to afternoon lessons.

"Oi!" Connor called to a passing Year 5 boy. "Want to help at the fair? We need people to run the hook-a-duck."

The boy barely slowed down. "Nah, I'm busy."

"Busy doing what?"

"Stuff." And he was gone.

"This is a disaster," Maya said flatly.

"It's not a disaster," Jamal said, though he was frowning at his notebook. "We still have four weeks. That's plenty of time to find volunteers."

"We need at least twelve people. For setup, running stalls, and cleanup. We've got us four, and that's it."

"Mrs. Sharma said some teachers might help."

"Might. And teachers have other things to do. We can't run a fair with four people and some teachers who might show up."

A group of Year 6 girls walked past, giggling about something to themselves.

"Sophie!" Maya called. "Do you want to..."

"Can't, sorry. I've got dance." Sophie didn't even break stride.

"Dance isn't until..." Maya started, but the girls had already rounded the corner.

Lily's shoulders slumped. "Why doesn't anyone want to help?"

It was a good question. The crew had spent so much time figuring out what activities to have, how to spend their budget, how to weigh costs and benefits. They'd never really thought about the people part. They'd just assumed that once the fair was planned, volunteers would appear.

They didn't.

"Let's think about this properly," Jamal said, in his solving-a-maths-problem voice. "Why would someone give up their Saturday to run a stall at a fair they're not even organising?"

"Because it's fun?" Lily offered.

"Is it, though? Standing behind a tombola table for four hours?"

"Because they're nice people who want to help the community?"

"Some people are. But clearly not enough, or the sheet wouldn't be empty."

"Because..." Connor trailed off. "Actually, I don't know. Why would anyone help with anything?"

They stood like rocks in a river, the corridor flowing around them.

"We need to give them a reason," Maya said finally. "Something that makes helping worth it."

"Like what?"

"I don't know. But there must be something. People volunteer for things all the time. We just need to figure out what makes them say yes."

. . . .

Operation Volunteer began at lunchtime the next day.

"Free food," Connor announced, slapping a new

poster next to their sign-up sheet. "That's what people want. Free stuff."

The poster read:

HELP AT THE FAIR → GET FREE FOOD ALL DAY!

"Where are we getting free food from?" Jamal asked.

"The cake stall. And whatever else we can scrounge. The point is, people love free things."

"We can't give away all the cake stall food. That's for selling. To raise money."

"Not all of it. Just enough to bribe, I mean to *encourage*, people to help."

By the end of lunch, three names had appeared on the sign-up sheet.

"See?" Connor was triumphant. "Free food works."

"Three people," Maya said. "We need twelve."

"It's only been an hour!"

But by the next morning, no new names had appeared. And one of the three, a Year 4 boy named Marcus, had crossed his name out with a note: Sorry, forgot I have football.

"Two people," Lily reported glumly. "We've gone backwards."

"We need a bigger reward," Connor decided. "Free food isn't enough. What about prizes?"

The new poster appeared that afternoon:

VOLUNTEERS GET ENTERED INTO A PRIZE DRAW! FIRST PRIZE: £20 GIFT CARD!

"Where are we getting £20 for a gift card?" Jamal asked, his eye twitching slightly.

"From the contingency fund. It's an investment."

"The contingency fund is for emergencies."

"This is an emergency. We have no volunteers."

Two more names appeared by the end of the day. One was Connor's younger cousin, who'd probably been threatened with something. The other was a girl named Priya from Year 5, who asked very specific questions about the odds of winning and seemed disappointed when she learned there would be other entrants.

"Four volunteers," Maya said, that evening in the treehouse. "Four people for twelve jobs."

"The incentives are working," Connor insisted. "Just slowly."

"Are they working? Or are we just getting people who want free stuff and might win money?"

"What's the difference?"

"The difference is..." Maya struggled to find the words to explain what she was feeling. "The people who signed up so far. Do they actually care about the fair?"

"Does it matter if they care? As long as they show up and do the job?"

"I think it might matter." Lily had been quiet, but now she looked up from her sketchbook. "My mum volunteers at the animal shelter. She doesn't get free food or prizes. She just... likes helping animals. And she's really good at it. Because she cares."

"So we need to find people who care about the fair?"

"Maybe. Or maybe we need to help people care?"

"That sounds harder than just giving them free stuff."

. . . .

Ten minutes passed with no one noticing Jamal's silence. Then a sudden outburst.

"Recognition," he said, presenting a carefully designed certificate. "People like being recognised for doing good things. What if we promise that all volunteers will be thanked publicly at the fair? Names announced, certificates presented, maybe even a photo in the local paper?"

"Would the local paper actually take a photo?" Maya asked.

"I don't know. But we could ask."

The new sign-up sheet featured the promise:

ALL VOLUNTEERS WILL BE PUBLICLY THANKED AND RECEIVE A CERTIFICATE OF APPRECIATION!

This worked better than the prizes had. By the end of the week, they had three more names: two Year 6 students who seemed keen on adding "community volunteer" to whatever mysterious records Year 6 students cared about, and a Year 3 girl named Amara who said her mum would be proud of her.

"Seven volunteers," Lily counted. "That's better."

"Still need five more," Maya said.

But then something strange happened.

Marcus, the boy who'd crossed his name off when football conflicted, appeared at their lunch table, looking uncomfortable.

"Is it true you're doing certificates?" he asked.

"Yes," Jamal said. "Why?"

"My sister heard about it. She said if I don't volunteer, she will, and then she'll have a certificate and I won't, and she'll never let me forget it."

"So... you want to sign up again?"

"I guess." He didn't sound thrilled. "But can you put me on something that ends before three? I really do have football at half three."

He signed up for setup and the first hour of the tombola, and left looking slightly resentful.

"That was weird," Connor said.

"Competition," Lily observed. "He doesn't want to help. He just doesn't want his sister to have something he doesn't."

"Is that... good?"

"I don't know. He'll show up, which is good. But he won't be happy about it."

. . . .

The problems with their approach became clearer over the following days.

First, Priya, the girl interested in prize draw odds, started asking whether volunteers who worked longer shifts would get more entries in the draw. When Maya said no, Priya announced she'd just do the minimum required and spend the rest of her time 'enjoying the fair properly'.

Then two of the Year 6 students got into an argument about whose name would be announced first during the thank-you ceremony. One of them threatened to withdraw entirely if he wasn't recognised as 'head volunteer'.

Then, worst of all, Maya's mum mentioned the volunteer situation to her friend Mrs. O'Leary (Lily's mum), who mentioned it to Mrs. Khan (Jamal's mum), who mentioned it at her book club, where apparently several parents had been considering volunteering anyway, just to be helpful.

"My mum says Mrs. Hill was going to sign up," Jamal reported, "but then she heard about the gift card and got annoyed. She said it felt like we were trying to pay people to do something they should do for free. Like we thought they wouldn't help unless there was something in it for them."

"But there is something in it for them," Connor protested. "Free food! Prizes! Certificates!"

"That's the problem. She was going to help because she wanted to. Now she feels like her wanting to help isn't worth as much as the people who only signed up for rewards."

Maya put her head in her hands. "We made it worse. We actually made it worse."

"Not worse, exactly..."

"We had four volunteers before. Now we have eight, but three of them are grumpy, one of them is only doing the minimum, and we've annoyed a bunch of adults who might have helped for free."

Even Connor had nothing to say to that.

"I don't understand," Connor said finally. "Rewards are supposed to make people want to do things. That's how it works. My parents give me extra screen time when I do chores. The school gives out house points for good behaviour. Everyone does this."

"But it's different somehow," Lily said slowly. She'd been drawing while they talked, figures on a page, some smiling, some frowning, arrows pointing in different directions. "When you reward someone for doing something, it changes what the thing means."

"Changes how?"

"Like..." Lily chewed her pencil thinking. "My mum at the animal shelter. If they started paying her, she'd probably still go. But it would feel different. It wouldn't be volunteering anymore. It would be a job."

"So? Jobs are fine."

"But she might enjoy it less. Even though she was getting money." Lily frowned at her own words, testing them. "Right now she goes because she wants to. If they paid her, she'd go because she was supposed to."

"What's the difference?"

"The money would kind of... replace the good feeling? Like... right now she goes because she wants to. If they paid her, maybe she'd go because she was supposed to. That's different, isn't it?"

Connor looked unconvinced, but he didn't argue.

Maya was nodding slowly. "Mrs. Hill was going to help anyway. And then we basically told her... what? That we didn't think she would? That we needed to pay her?"

"We didn't say that."

"We kind of did, though. By offering the gift card."

Maya stared at the table. "Like her wanting to help wasn't enough."

Connor looked genuinely confused. "So... rewards are bad? We shouldn't offer anything?"

"Not exactly." Maya was thinking hard. "Priya signed up for the prize draw, and she wouldn't have signed up otherwise. The rewards got us some volunteers we wouldn't have had. It's just... they also got us volunteers who don't really care, and they pushed away people who would have helped for different reasons."

"Different reasons like what?"

"Like caring. Like wanting to be part of something. Like enjoying the feeling of helping." Lily held up her sketch. The figures were clearer now. Some had pound signs for eyes, reaching for a prize. Others had hearts, reaching toward each other. "Different people want different things. Some people want rewards. Some people want to feel good about themselves. Some people want to belong to something."

"And we've been treating everyone like the pound-sign people," Maya finished. "When loads of them might be heart people. If we asked differently."

. . . .

The crew spent the next afternoon at the kitchen table in Maya's house, redesigning their entire approach.

"Two tracks," Maya said, writing on a large sheet of paper. "We keep some of the reward stuff for people who need it. But we also create a different kind of appeal for people who just want to help."

"Like what?"

"Community. Belonging. Being part of making something good happen." She wrote: THE MILLBROOK SPIRIT TEAM.

"What's the Millbrook Spirit Team?"

"Us. And anyone who wants to join." Maya was getting excited now. "We invite people to be part of saving a tradition. Part of something that matters."

"That's just... words," Connor said sceptically.

"Words matter. The way you ask changes what people feel they're saying yes to."

Jamal was nodding. "My dad talks about this at work. He says when they want people to work extra hours, they can either offer overtime pay or tell people the project really matters and the team needs them. Different people respond to different messages."

"So we send different messages to different people?"

"Sort of. We make it clear there are different ways to be involved, and different reasons to help."

Maya was writing fast now. "The prize draw stays; some people need that. But we also have the Spirit Team for people who want to feel like they're part of something. We have the family volunteer option for parents who want to help alongside their kids. We have the 'doing it for Millbrook' angle for people who care about the community."

"And the certificates?"

"We keep those too. Some people like recognition. But we'll make it about celebrating contributions, not ranking who did most."

Lily had started a new drawing. A circular diagram with the fair in the middle and different types of people around the edges, each with different arrows pointing toward the centre.

"Different reasons to help for different motivations," she said.

"Exactly." Maya sat back. "We can't make everyone care about the same things. But we can make sure that whatever they care about, they have a reason to help."

. . . .

The new approach rolled out on Monday.

The old poster came down. In its place went three different sheets:

THE MILLBROOK SPIRIT TEAM

Help save a Millbrook tradition! Join the team making history. First meeting Thursday lunch. Everyone welcome.

FAMILY VOLUNTEER DAY

Help with your child! Setup Saturday morning, 8-10am. Parents and kids working together.

WANT TO EARN REWARDS?

Help at the fair. Enter the prize draw. Free food all day!

"That last one's basically what we had before," Connor observed.

"For the people who want what we had before. We're just adding other options to it."

The Spirit Team meeting on Thursday drew seven new people, a mix of students who seemed genuinely excited about the fair being "their" project. Lily led the meeting, talking about the history of the Millbrook Fair, about Maya's grandmother's memories, about what it would mean to prove that young people could make something wonderful happen.

The Family Volunteer signup brought in four parents who wanted to help their children, including (to everyone's relief) Mrs. Hill, who said she was glad to see they weren't "treating everyone like hired help anymore."

And the reward poster? It still attracted a few people. Priya was still only doing minimum hours. The Year 6 boy still wanted to be called "head volunteer." But now they were part of a larger group with others who were there for different reasons.

"We've got nineteen people," Jamal announced by the end of the week. "More than we need."

"We've got a waiting list!" Connor said gleefully.

But Maya noticed something else: the quality of help had changed. The Spirit Team members showed up to planning meetings with ideas. The family volunteers started a group to coordinate. Even some of the reward-seeking people seemed to be catching enthusiasm from everyone else.

"It's contagious," Lily observed. "When some people really care, it makes other people care more too."

"Is that an incentive?" Connor asked. "Catching caring from other people?"

"Maybe the best kind."

That evening, Maya sat with her grandmother on the sofa, showing her pictures of the planning meetings, the Spirit Team, the growing volunteer list.

"All these people," Gran said, with wonder in her voice. "All helping with the fair."

"Different people for different reasons," Maya explained. "Some want prizes. Some want to feel good about helping. Some just want to be part of something."

"And you figured all that out yourselves?"

"We got it wrong first. We thought everyone wanted the same things. Turns out people are more complicated than that."

Gran smiled, her weathered hand covering Maya's. "That's a lesson some people never learn. That what makes one person tick isn't what makes another person tick. And if you want people to do something, really want them to, with their whole hearts, you have to understand what they actually care about."

"Is that what you learned from the old fairs?"

"From life, really. But the fairs helped." Gran's eyes went distant, remembering. "Your grandfather used to run the raffle. Worst salesman you ever met. Couldn't convince anyone to buy a ticket if their life depended on it. But he could convince anyone to donate a prize. Do you know why?"

Maya shook her head.

"Because he didn't ask them to give something away. He asked them to be part of making the fair wonderful. He'd tell them about the children who'd line up, the excitement of the draw, the joy on the winner's face. He made them feel that their donation mattered. That they mattered." Gran patted Maya's hand. "The prizes weren't the point. The belonging was the point. The prizes just gave people a way in."

Maya thought about that as she helped Gran to bed, as she brushed her teeth and put on her pyjamas and lay in the dark thinking about incentives and motivations and all the complicated ways that people decided to do things.

Different people wanted different things. That was the part she hadn't understood before. She'd thought there was one way to ask, one kind of reason that would work for everyone.

But Mrs. Hill wasn't Priya. The Spirit Team kids weren't the prize-draw people. And somehow, once you saw that, you could find ways to help each of them say yes.

Three weeks until the fair. Nineteen volunteers and counting. And for the first time, Maya felt like they had an actual team.

Because they'd given people something worth being a part of.

Chapter Four Activities

Discussion Questions

1. The Crew tried offering free food and prizes to get volunteers, but Mrs. Hill was annoyed because she'd been planning to help anyway. Why do you think rewards might actually put some people OFF helping?

2. Marcus only signed up because his sister was going to and he didn't want her to have a certificate he didn't have. Is that a good reason to volunteer? Does it matter why someone helps, as long as they help?

3. Lily drew some people with pound signs for eyes (wanting rewards) and some with hearts (wanting to belong). Which type of person would you rather have helping at an event? Why?

4. Gran said Maya's grandfather didn't ask people to "give something away", he asked them to "be part of making the fair wonderful." What's the difference? How does the way you ask change how people feel about helping?

5. The Spirit Team approach worked better than prizes. But does that mean prizes are always wrong? Can you think of times when a reward IS the right way to encourage someone?

Quick Activities

Activity 1: What Makes YOU Want to Help?

Time: 5 minutes

Rank these from 1 (most motivating) to 5 (least motivating):

- Getting a reward (prize, money, treat)
- Being thanked and recognised publicly
- Feeling like part of a team
- Helping someone I care about
- Just knowing I did something good

Now think:

- Would your ranking change depending on what you were being asked to help with?
- Do you think your friends would rank these the same way you did?

Activity 2: Rewrite the Poster

Time: 10 minutes

The Crew's first volunteer poster focused on rewards. Their later approach focused on belonging and community. Try rewriting these "reward" messages to focus on something else:

1. Original: "Help at the fair and win a £20 gift card!"

Your version:

2. Original: "Volunteers get free food all day!"

Your version:

3. Original: "Help clean up and get a certificate!"

Your version:

Challenge: Can you write a poster that would appeal to BOTH pound-sign people AND heart people?

Activity 3: Pound-Sign or Heart?

Time: 10 minutes

For each scenario below, decide: Is this person more of a "pound-sign person" or a "heart person"? Or something else entirely?

- Aisha helps her neighbour carry shopping because "it's the right thing to do."
- Ben tidies his room when his mum offers extra screen time.
- Chloe volunteers at the shelter because she loves animals.
- Daniel joins the school council because it will look good on his report.
- Emma helps with the school play because all her friends are doing it.
- Finn organises a charity run because his grandma had the illness they're raising money for.

Discuss: Are any of these motivations "wrong"? Does it matter WHY someone does a good thing, as long as they do it?

Extended Activities

Extended Activity 1: The Motivation Detective

Time: Ongoing over one week

1. Over the next week, keep an eye out for times when someone tries to get you (or others) to do something. This could be parents, teachers, adverts, or friends.
2. Each time you notice one, write down: What did they want people to do? How did they try to encourage it? (Reward? Recognition? Making it fun? Making it feel important?)
3. At the end of the week, look at your list. Which approaches worked best? Did any backfire like the Crew's prize poster?

Things to look out for:

- School reward systems (house points, merits, prizes)
- Adverts ("Buy one get one free!", "Join the club!")
- Parents ("If you finish your homework, you can...", "It would really help me if...")
- Friends ("Come on, it'll be fun!", "Everyone's doing it!")

Extended Activity 2: Design Your Own Spirit Team

Time: 30-45 minutes

The Crew's "Millbrook Spirit Team" gave people a sense of belonging and purpose. Now design your own!

1. Think of something at your school or in your community that could use volunteers. (Library helpers? Playground buddies? Litter picking? Helping younger children read?)
2. Give your volunteer group a name that makes it sound exciting and important (like "Spirit Team" or "The Millbrook Crew").
3. Design a poster that appeals to "heart people". Focus on belonging, making a difference, and being part of something special.
4. Now design a second poster for the same thing, but aimed at "pound-sign people". Focus on rewards, recognition, or benefits.
5. Show both posters to friends or family. Which one would make THEM want to join? Why?

Bonus: If your school actually needs volunteers for something, ask a teacher if you could try your recruitment approach for real!

Extended Activity 3: The Reward Experiment

Time: Set up in 15 minutes, observe over 2 weeks

Mrs. Hill was going to help anyway, but felt put off when rewards were offered. Scientists have actually studied this! Try your own experiment:

1. Pick something you already enjoy doing (reading, drawing, playing an instrument, a sport).
2. For one week, do this activity as normal. At the end of each day, rate how much you enjoyed it from 1–10.
3. For the second week, give yourself a small reward every time you do the activity (a treat, screen time, a sticker. Something you like).
4. Again, rate your enjoyment 1–10 each day.
5. Compare your scores. Did adding a reward make the activity MORE enjoyable, LESS enjoyable, or about the same?

Think about:

- Did you start thinking about the reward more than the activity itself?
- What happened to your motivation when you thought about NOT getting the reward?
- Would you want to do this activity during a third week with NO reward? How would that feel?

Chapter 5 Parent/Educator Guide

Concept: Marginal Analysis

Marginal analysis asks: "What's the benefit of one more unit, compared to its cost?" Each additional unit typically provides less satisfaction than the one before. Economists call this 'diminishing marginal utility'. The first biscuit is delicious. The sixth might make you feel sick.

In a Child's World

Children experience this constantly: the first Christmas toy brings more excitement than the tenth. They face marginal decisions daily: "Should I have one more sweet?" "Should I stay up for one more chapter?" This chapter helps them evaluate whether additional benefits justify additional costs.

In Your World

Adults apply marginal thinking often without labelling it through budgets ("Can we afford one more expense?"), time management, and projects. The concept underpins the crucial wisdom that more isn't always better, and knowing when to stop matters as much as knowing when to start.

Why it Matters

Marginal analysis helps children resist the temptation of "just one more". It also implicitly introduces the value of contingency. Children who learn these ideas make more considered decisions, and are better prepared for a world where things don't always go to plan.

5

Just One More?

One week until the fair.

Maya was in the middle of the school field with her checklist, ticking things off as she walked. Coconut shy frame: ready, stored in the PE shed. Tombola drum: borrowed from the church hall, cleaned and tested. Face painting supplies: delivered, sorted into Lily's carefully labelled boxes. Hook-a-duck: Connor had built the trough himself, and it held water without leaking, which was more of an achievement than Maya had realised.

Everything was coming together. Eight activities confirmed. Nineteen volunteers trained and scheduled. £101 remaining in the budget. They'd actually come in under their target by finding a cheaper supplier for tombola prizes.

"We might actually pull this off," she said to no one in particular.

"Don't jinx it," Connor called from across the field, where he was pacing out distances for the welly wanging pitch. "My nan says you should never celebrate before it's actually happened."

"I'm not celebrating. I'm just... cautiously optimistic."

"That's what people say right before everything goes wrong."

Maya ignored him and kept walking. The field looked different when she imagined it full of stalls and people, transformed from an ordinary rectangle of grass into the Millbrook Kids' Fair, the thing they'd been working toward for eight weeks.

Seven weeks of planning. Countless meetings. Arguments about bouncy castles and whether numbers could make decisions. And now, somehow, they were nearly there.

Her phone buzzed. Jamal.

Emergency meeting. Treehouse. Now.

Maya's cautious optimism evaporated instantly.

. . . .

"It's not an emergency emergency," Jamal said, once they'd all climbed up and settled into their spots. "It's more of an... opportunity."

"You said emergency," Connor pointed out.

"I panicked. I didn't want anyone to miss it."

"Miss what?"

Jamal pulled out his phone and showed them a message. It was from Mrs. Sharma, forwarded from someone Maya didn't recognise.

> *Dear Mrs. Sharma,*
>
> *I understand your students are organising a community fair. My company, Bounce Kingdom, is running a promotion this month: 25% off all bouncy castle hires for charity and school events. This would bring our small castle rental to just £60 for four hours.*
>
> *If you're interested, please book by Thursday as slots are filling quickly.*
>
> *Kind regards,*
> *Marcus Webb*
> *Bounce Kingdom Ltd.*

The treehouse went very quiet.

"£60," Lily breathed. "That's a great deal!"

"We have £101 in contingency," Jamal said. "If we spent £60 on the bouncy castle, we'd still have £41 left for actual emergencies."

"A bouncy castle," Connor said, a grin spreading across his face. "An actual bouncy castle. We could have one after all."

Maya felt the pull of it. The excitement, the

possibility. A bouncy castle would transform the fair. It would be the first thing people saw, the thing children would talk about afterwards.

But something held her back.

"We already decided against the bouncy castle," she said slowly. "Remember? Costs outweighed benefits."

"That was when it cost £80," Connor argued. "Now it costs £60. The costs are 25% lower than what they were."

"The other costs haven't changed, though. It still takes up loads of space. Still needs supervision. Still needs electricity..."

"We already have the generator for the music."

"It still needs someone watching it all day."

"We have nineteen volunteers! We're turning people away!"

Maya looked at Jamal. "What do you think?"

Jamal was pulling the face he did when the numbers were fighting with the feelings in his head. "The cost has changed. That changes the calculation. But..." He paused. "I don't know. It feels different from our other decisions."

"Different how?"

"We made a plan. We stuck to the plan. The plan works." Jamal was frowning, trying to work something out. "Now we're asking whether to add something extra. Something we already decided against."

"But the price changed," Connor said.

"I know. But..." Jamal struggled for words. "It feels different. Before, we were building the fair from nothing. Now the fair exists. It's already good."

"So?"

"So adding the bouncy castle isn't about making the fair possible. It's about making it... I don't know. Better? But also riskier. We'd have less backup money. More things to manage. In the last week."

"You're saying the question isn't 'is a bouncy castle good?' It's 'is a bouncy castle good now, with everything else we've got?'"

"Yeah." Jamal looked relieved. "Yeah, that's right."

Connor slumped. "So we're not getting it."

"I didn't say that. I said we should think about it properly. Like we've thought about everything else."

They spent the next hour applying their now-familiar process to the bouncy castle question.

The benefits of adding it: excitement, impressiveness, something for younger children, visual centrepiece.

The costs of adding it: £60 from contingency, supervision needs, space requirements, setup complexity, last-minute coordination stress.

But this time, Maya noticed something different about the discussion. They weren't comparing the bouncy castle to nothing. They were comparing the fair *with* a bouncy castle to the fair *without* one.

"The fair's already good," Lily said quietly. "We've got eight activities. People are excited. Volunteers are ready. If we add the bouncy castle and something goes wrong..."

"Like what?" Connor demanded.

"I don't know. That's the point of contingency. Things you don't expect."

"Nothing's going to go wrong."

"You can't know that."

"I can hope that."

"Hope isn't a plan."

They stared at each other across the cable-reel table, the bouncy castle hovering between. A question no one could quite answer.

"Let's vote," Maya said finally. "All in favour of adding

the bouncy castle?"

Connor's hand shot up immediately. After a moment, Lily raised hers too, though she looked uncertain.

"Against?"

Jamal raised his hand. Maya hesitated, then raised hers as well.

"Tied," Connor said. "Great. Now what?"

Maya looked at the notebook in front of her, at the weeks of decisions recorded in her handwriting. They'd come so far by thinking carefully, by not just grabbing at things they wanted.

"Let me ask a different question," she said. "If we weren't sitting here with £101 in contingency, if we only had £65 left, would we even consider the bouncy castle?"

"No," Jamal said immediately. "We'd keep the money for emergencies."

"So the only reason we're considering it is because we have extra money. Not because the fair needs it."

"That's not..." Connor started, then stopped. "Actually, that makes sense. The fair doesn't need it. I just want it."

"I want it too," Maya admitted. "But wanting something isn't the same as it being the right choice."

Lily had been sketching again. Two versions of the

fair, one with a bouncy castle, one without. They looked almost identical, Maya realised. The bouncy castle version had something extra, but the other version wasn't empty or incomplete.

"We should keep the money," Lily said finally. "The fair's already good. We don't need it."

"But we want it," Connor said.

"I know. I want it too." Lily looked at her lap. "But what if something goes wrong? What if we need that money for something we can't even imagine yet?"

"Nothing's going to go wrong."

"You don't know that."

The vote changed. Three against, one in favour.

Connor looked genuinely disappointed, but he didn't argue. "Fine. No bouncy castle. But if nothing goes wrong and we end up with £101 left over, I reserve the right to say I told you so."

"Noted," Maya said. "Now let's focus on making the fair we actually planned as good as it can possibly be."

. . . .

Then, on Friday, something went wrong.

Maya woke to rain hammering against her window. A heavy, relentless downpour you could tell meant business. She grabbed her phone and checked the weather app.

Saturday: Heavy rain throughout the day.
90% chance of precipitation.
High winds possible in afternoon.

Her heart sank.
The group chat was already exploding:

Connor: *Have you SEEN the forecast!?*
Lily: *Maybe it will change?*
Jamal: *Weather forecasts for tomorrow are usually accurate.*
Connor: *We're doomed.*
Lily: *We're not doomed!*
Connor: *DOOMED*

Maya typed quickly: *Emergency meeting. My house. One hour.*

. . . .

By mid-morning, the Millbrook Crew was crowded around Maya's kitchen table, rain still streaming down the windows behind them. Mrs. Patterson had provided hot chocolate and then wisely slipped away to leave them to it.

"Options," Maya said, forcing her voice to stay calm. "What are our options?"

"Cancel," Connor said glumly. "Tell everyone it's off, try again next year."

"We can't cancel. The council's coming to evaluate. If we cancel, Councillor Davies wins. He was right all along. Kids can't organise things."

"Then we do it in the rain. People will just get wet."

"In heavy rain and high winds? Nobody will come. The tombola tickets will dissolve. The face paint will wash off. The welly wanging will be.. actually, welly wanging in mud might be quite good."

"Focus," Jamal said. "What else?"

Lily had been quiet, staring at something on her phone. "What if we move it indoors?"

"Indoors where? The school hall's not big enough for eight activities."

"Not the school." Lily turned her phone around. "The church hall. St. Michael's. It's right across from the field. My mum knows the vicar."

"Would they let us use it?"

"I don't know. But we could ask."

Maya thought about the church hall. She'd been there for jumble sales and community events. It was old, with a slightly musty smell and terrible lighting. But it was also big. Big enough, maybe.

"What would we lose?" she asked. "If we moved indoors?"

Jamal was already making notes. "Welly wanging. Can't do that inside. Coconut shy. Probably too dangerous. But the tombola, face painting, hook-a-duck, cake stall, guess-the-sweeties, splat-the-rat... those could all work."

"That's six out of eight activities."

"Six activities in a dry hall versus eight activities in a storm," Lily said. "I know which I'd choose."

"What about the volunteers? The setup? Everything's planned for the field."

"We have" Jamal checked his phone. "Nineteen hours before the fair starts. And £101 in contingency."

"What would the money be for?"

"I don't know. Renting the hall, maybe? Buying extra supplies? Whatever we need to make the move work."

Connor was shaking his head in disbelief. "Yesterday we were arguing about bouncy castles. Today we're trying to save the whole fair."

"Good thing we didn't spend the money on the

bouncy castle, then," Maya said, and watched as the realisation hit Connor.

"Oh." Connor blinked. "Yeah."

. . . .

The next four hours were the most intense of Maya's life.

Lily called her mum, who called the vicar, who called back to say the hall was available tomorrow. They'd had a wedding rehearsal cancel, but would need a £50 deposit and the hall would need to be cleaned up thoroughly afterward.

Maya drafted a message for the volunteer group, explaining the change and asking who could still help with the new plan. Sixteen of the nineteen responded within an hour. All sixteen said yes.

Connor and Jamal went to the church hall to measure and plan, and came back with a hand-drawn layout showing where each activity could go.

Mrs. Patterson drove them to the school to collect the supplies they'd stored in the PE shed, then to the church hall to drop everything off. The vicar, a young woman named Rev. Patricia, helped them stack boxes and seemed genuinely excited about the fair.

"We don't get many young people planning events," she said. "It's wonderful to see."

"We didn't plan for rain," Maya admitted.

By evening, the new plan was in place. Smaller, different, missing two activities, but happening nonetheless.

Maya stood in the church hall as the light faded, looking at the empty space that would tomorrow be full of stalls and people and children with painted faces.

"We spent £45," Jamal reported, checking his phone. "£50 for the hall deposit, but Rev. Patricia waived £5 because she liked our 'vibe.' We have £56 left."

"£56."

"And a fair."

"And a fair."

They stood in silence for a moment, the weight of the week settling around them.

"This isn't what we planned," Lily's voice was barely above a whisper.

"No," Maya agreed. "But it's something."

"Do you think Councillor Davies will be impressed?"

"I don't know. But we'll have done our best with what we had. That's all we could ever do."

. . . .

Saturday, 10:47 AM. The Millbrook Kids' Fair.

The church hall had never looked like this before.

Lily's decorations transformed the space. Bunting in bright colours strung between the old wooden beams, hand-painted signs pointing to each activity, a banner over the entrance reading WELCOME TO THE MILLBROOK KIDS' FAIR in letters that looked joyfully homemade.

The tombola drum sat on a table draped in red cloth, already spinning as children reached in for numbered tickets. The hook-a-duck trough took up one corner, plastic ducks bobbing cheerfully while a Year 3 volunteer helped smaller children with their fishing rods. Face painting had a queue stretching halfway across the hall. Lily had recruited two friends from the art club to help, and they'd set up three stations to handle the demand.

The cake stall had sold out of brownies within the first hour. The splat-the-rat was causing shrieks of laughter every few minutes. The guess-the-sweeties jar had collected over forty entries, each guess more wildly optimistic than the last.

And the people. So many people.

Maya hadn't expected this many. Word had spread about the venue change. Parents arrived with umbrellas and sympathy and ended up staying for hours. Teachers from school stopped by, including Mrs.

Sharma, who bought three raffle tickets and told everyone within earshot how proud she was.

"This is amazing," Connor said, finding Maya near the entrance. "We actually did it."

"We're not done yet." But Maya was smiling. "Three more hours to go."

"Three more hours of success."

"Don't jinx it."

"You sound like my nan."

Maya laughed, for what felt like the first time in weeks. And then froze.

Councillor Davies had just walked through the door.

He stood in the entrance, rain dripping from his umbrella, his eyes moving slowly across the hall. Taking in the decorations. The queues. The laughter. The children with tiger faces and butterfly cheeks running past him toward the hook-a-duck.

Maya straightened her shoulders and walked toward him.

"Councillor Davies. Welcome to the Millbrook Kids' Fair."

He didn't smile. His eyes kept scanning the room, evaluating, judging, doing whatever it was that council representatives did.

"I heard you had to move venues," he said finally.

"Yes. The weather..."

"I know about the weather." He was still looking around. "I assumed you'd cancel."

"We considered it. But we'd made commitments. To our volunteers. To the people who believed we could do this."

"So you moved everything in..." He checked his watch. "Nineteen hours?"

"Sixteen, by the time we finished planning. Nineteen from when we found out about the forecast."

For a long moment, Councillor Davies said nothing. Then he reached into his coat pocket and pulled out a small notebook, leather-bound, official-looking, and wrote something down.

"The budget," he said. "How much did you spend?"

"£99 on planned activities. £50 to rent this hall at the last minute. £5 refunded by the vicar. We have £56 remaining."

"You came in under budget."

"Yes."

"Even with the emergency."

"The contingency helped. We had money saved for unexpected problems."

Another note in the notebook. Another long look around the hall.

"I was wrong," Councillor Davies said.

Maya blinked. "Sorry?"

"I said children don't understand money. That you'd prove the fair was a luxury we couldn't afford." He tucked the notebook back in his pocket. "You proved the opposite. You had a plan, and when the plan fell apart, you made a new one. In nineteen hours."

He looked around the hall again. The bunting. The queues. The laughter.

"Most adults would have cancelled," he said. "You adapted."

Maya didn't know what to say. This wasn't the Councillor Davies from the council meeting; sarcastic, dismissive, and confident that they'd fail.

"The Millbrook Fair," he continued. "The full one. The council will reconsider the cancellation. I'll recommend we reinstate it for next year, with a planning committee that includes..." He paused, the ghost of a smile crossing his face. "Youth representatives. If you're interested."

"We're interested," Maya managed. "We're definitely

interested."

"Good." He looked at his watch again. "Now, if you'll excuse me, I believe I saw a cake stall, and I haven't had breakfast."

He walked off toward the baked goods, leaving Maya standing alone in the entrance, rain still pattering against the windows.

They'd done it. They'd actually pulled it off.

. . . .

The last visitor arrived at 2:34 PM, twenty-six minutes before closing.

Maya spotted her grandmother the moment she came through the door, walking slowly with her cane.

"Gran!" Maya ran across the hall, dodging a face-painted superhero and nearly colliding with the tombola table. "You came!"

"Did you think I'd miss it?" Gran's eyes were bright, taking in everything. "Oh, Maya. Look at this. Look at what you've made."

"It's not the field. And there's no bouncy castle, and the coconut shy didn't fit, and..."

"Hush." Gran squeezed her hand. "It's perfect. It's absolutely perfect."

"It's not what I imagined."

"The best things never are. You know what I remember most about the old fairs? Not the carousels or the toffee apples. I remember the feeling. The sense that the whole village had come together to make something special." She looked around again, her smile deepening. "That's what I feel here. You've got the spirit of it. The heart."

Maya felt tears prickling at her eyes and blinked them back fiercely. "Do you want to see everything? The tombola's nearly finished but there might be prizes left, and Lily's doing face painting, and..."

"Take me around," Gran said. "Show me your fair."

They walked through the hall together, slowly, Gran's cane tapping on the wooden floor. Maya pointed out each activity, sharing the story behind it. Here's the hook-a-duck that Connor built. Here's the splat-the-rat that Jamal designed. Here's the sweetie jar that has 347 sweets... Pretend you didn't hear that..."

Gran listened to everything. Asked questions. Laughed at the right moments. When they reached the face painting station, she insisted on getting a butterfly on her hand. "Small, dear, I'm not as flamboyant as I used to be." She showed it to everyone she passed.

"Your grandfather would have loved this," she said, as they completed their circuit. "He always said the fair was about bringing people together."

"We nearly didn't make it," Maya admitted. "So many times, it almost fell apart."

"But it didn't."

"No." Maya looked around at the hall. The bunting,

the queues, the faces. "I don't know exactly why. We just... kept figuring things out. One problem at a time."

Gran nodded slowly. "Most people never learn what you've learned this summer."

"What's that?"

Gran was quiet for a moment, watching a child run past with a tiger face and a tombola prize clutched in each hand.

"That choosing is hard," she said finally. "And that choosing well is harder. But it's worth learning how."

The hall was starting to empty now, families gathering their things, children protesting that they didn't want to leave. The rain had finally stopped, late afternoon sunlight breaking through the clouds that remained, casting everything in gold.

"I have something for you," Gran said. She reached into her handbag and pulled out a piece of paper, old, faded, and folded into careful squares. "I found it last week. I was going to give it to you at the real fair, but..."

Maya took the paper and unfolded it gently. It was a poster. Hand-drawn, with colours that had faded to pastels over decades.

MILLBROOK VILLAGE FAIR - 1962
SATURDAY, SEPTEMBER 15TH
CAROUSEL - COCONUT SHY - TOMBOLA.
ALL WELCOME!

"That was the first fair I ever went to," Gran said softly. "I was nine years old. Your age, near enough. My father helped paint the signs. My mother ran the cake stall. The whole village came together, just like today."

Maya stared at the poster, at the faded illustration of a carousel horse, at the hand-lettered words promising a day of joy.

"It's beautiful."

"It's yours now. A reminder of where this all started. And of what you've helped continue."

Maya hugged her grandmother, and didn't try to blink back the tears this time.

. . . .

Cleanup took longer than expected. The Spirit Team stayed until the last chair was stacked, the last table wiped down, the last piece of bunting carefully wound around a cardboard tube for next time.

Next time. There would be a next time. Councillor Davies had all but promised.

As the crew walked home through the damp streets, the setting sun painting the clouds orange and pink, Maya felt something she couldn't quite name. Pride, yes. Relief, certainly. But something else too, something quieter and deeper.

"We spent £144," Jamal said, because he couldn't help himself. "£56 left over. We'll donate it to the church hall fund. Rev. Patricia said they need new heating."

"We had four hundred and twelve visitors," Lily added. "I counted. Well, estimated."

"We made £87 from activities," Connor contributed. "That goes to the school community fund. Mrs. Sharma nearly cried when we told her."

Maya listened to the numbers, proof that they'd actually done it, but her mind was elsewhere. On her grandmother's face when she saw the fair. On Councillor Davies' unexpected praise. On the feeling of standing in the hall that morning, watching something they'd imagined become something real.

"It wasn't what we planned," she said. "Not even close. But..."

"But it was good," Lily finished. "It was really good."

"Because we adapted," Jamal said. "We knew how to think about it. So when everything changed, we could... figure it out again. The same way."

"Also because we didn't buy the bouncy castle," Connor said. "I'm officially admitting you were right. The contingency saved us."

"I'm marking this day on my calendar," Maya said. "Connor Murphy admitting someone else was right."

"Don't get used to it."

They reached the corner where their paths separated. Connor heading north, Jamal east, Lily south, Maya west. For a moment, they stood in a loose circle, the same four people who'd sat in a treehouse eight weeks ago with a crumpled council notice and a mission.

"Same time next year?" Connor asked.

"Same time next year," Maya agreed.

"But bigger."

"But better," Lily corrected. "Bigger isn't always better, though. Remember the bouncy castle?"

"Better, then. The best Kids' Fair Millbrook has ever seen."

They split apart, heading home through the golden evening, the taste of success still fresh and the promise of next year already taking shape in their minds.

Maya walked slowly, savouring the moment. In her pocket, the faded poster crinkled gently. In her heart, something had shifted, something she couldn't quite name but knew she'd carry with her.

The Millbrook Fair would return next September. And next time, they'd know what they were doing.

Well. They'd know a bit more, anyway.

Maya smiled and kept walking.

Chapter Five Activities

Discussion Questions

1. When the bouncy castle offer came at £60 instead of £80, the Crew was tempted to add it. Connor said "I just want it." Is wanting something a good enough reason to change a plan you've already made?

2. Maya asked: "If we only had £65 left, would we even consider the bouncy castle?" Why was this question so important? How did it help them decide?

3. The Crew decided to keep their contingency money. Then the rain came and they needed it for the church hall. Was that just lucky? Or was it good planning?

4. Councillor Davies said "Most adults would have cancelled." Why do you think the Crew didn't give up? What made them keep going when everything went wrong?

5. Gran's poster from 1962 showed a fair with just a carousel, coconut shy, and tombola. The Crew's fair had six activities. Is more always better? What makes an event special?

Quick Activities

Activity 1: The "Just One More" Test

Time: 5 minutes

Here's a way to think through "just one more" decisions

For each scenario, ask yourself these three questions:

1. What am I giving up to get this one extra thing?
2. Is what I already have "good enough"?
3. What could go wrong if I use up my backup/savings?

Scenarios:

- You've packed a great lunch, but there's room for one more biscuit (your last one).
- You've saved enough for the toy you wanted, but there's an accessory pack that costs your last £5.
- Your homework is done, but you could add one more paragraph to make it longer.

Activity 2: Plan B Brainstorm

Time: 10 minutes

When the rain forecast appeared, the Crew didn't panic, they made a new plan. In 3 minutes, write down as many "Plan B" options as you can for the following scenarios:

Scenario 1: You've planned a picnic in the park with friends. Suddenly it starts raining.

Scenario 2: You've been working on a poster for school and accidentally spill water on it.

Notice: Good "Plan B" thinking means you don't waste time being upset, you jump straight to "What can I do now?"

Activity 3: The Contingency Calculator

Time: 10 minutes

The Crew kept £101 as contingency money for unexpected problems. Let's practice thinking about contingencies!

Scenario: You're planning a birthday party with a £50 budget.

1. List 5 things that could go wrong at a birthday party (weather, someone drops the cake, decorations break, etc.).
2. For each problem, estimate how much money you might need to fix it.
3. How much contingency would you keep from your £50 budget?
4. Now plan the party with what's left. Is it still a good party?

Think about: Is it better to have a slightly smaller party with backup money, or a bigger party with no safety net?

Extended Activities

Extended Activity 1: Your Own Fair Plan

Time: 45 minutes to 1 hour

Now that you've seen how the Crew planned their fair, try planning your own event! This brings together everything from the whole book.

Your challenge: Plan a fundraising event for your school or a cause you care about. You have £100 and one afternoon.

1. Brainstorm: List every activity you could include. Don't worry about cost yet
2. Research: Find out roughly how much each activity would cost. Cross out anything over £100 on its own.
3. Compare: Make a Good Points/Bad Points grid for your best 5 options.
4. Choose: Pick your final activities. Remember what you're giving up!
5. Plan volunteers: How would you ask people to help? Write a message or poster.
6. Keep contingency: Leave at least £15 unspent for emergencies.

Final questions:

- What was the hardest part of planning?
- What would you do if it rained on your event day?
- Would you actually want to run this event for real?

Extended Activity 2: The Emergency Response Challenge
Time: 30 minutes (can be done with friends or family)

The Crew had 19 hours to completely change their plans when rain threatened the fair. How fast can you adapt?

1. Get a timer and a partner (or do this alone).
2. Your partner gives you a "disaster scenario" for an event you're planning. (Examples: "The cake got dropped," "The main entertainer is sick," "The venue flooded.")
3. You have 5 minutes to come up with a complete Plan B. Write down: What will you do instead? Who needs to be told? What resources do you need? What will you say to guests?
4. Swap roles and try again with a different disaster.

Disaster ideas to try:

- Your birthday party venue double-booked and cancelled on you
- Half the food for your bake sale went mouldy
- The electricity went out during your movie night
- Your school play's costumes got lost in the post

Extended Activity 3: Interview
Time: 20 minutes

Councillor Davies was impressed that the Crew could explain their decisions. Can you explain yours?

1. Find a grown-up (parent, grandparent, teacher) who's willing to interview you about the book.
2. They ask you these questions:

    - "What did the Millbrook Crew learn about making choices?"
    - "What's a 'hidden cost' and can you give me an example?"
    - "How do you compare two options fairly?"
    - "Why didn't everyone want to volunteer at first? What changed?"
    - "Why is it important to keep some money in reserve?"
    - "What would you do differently if you were planning the fair?"

3. Ask the grown-up: "Did I explain it clearly? Could you understand what I meant? How could I Improve my answer"

About the Millbrook Town Adventures

Why Economic Literacy Matters

Every day, children make dozens of decisions: how to spend pocket money, what to trade at lunch, whether to save for something special or buy it now. These childhood choices are the foundation of economic thinking.

Economic literacy helps children recognise patterns in the world around them. Why do things cost what they do? Why can't we have everything we want? How do our choices affect others? What motivates people to make the decisions they make?

Children who understand economic principles become adults who make thoughtful decisions. They recognise trade-offs and opportunity costs in their lives. They understand how systems work, from their household to their community to their country. They think critically about policies, news, and the world they're inheriting.

These are life skills every child deserves.

The Storytelling Approach

We teach through the characters' experiences.

When Maya faces a difficult choice about the Millbrook Fair, she feels the weight of opportunity cost. When Jamal creates his budget table, he uses cost-benefit analysis to solve a problem that matters to him. The concepts emerge naturally from authentic struggles.

Research shows that children learn abstract concepts best when they encounter them within meaningful contexts. Stories provide that context. They create emotional stakes that make concepts memorable. They show consequences without preaching. They let children discover economic principles through observation and experience.

The Millbrook books never explain economics explicitly. Your child absorbs these concepts the same way they absorb grammar rules, through immersion rather than instruction. The activities at the end of each chapter reinforce their understanding of the concepts they meet.

The Millbrook Town Approach

All our stories take place in Millbrook, a fictional UK town where economic concepts are woven into everyday life. This consistent setting serves several purposes.

Familiarity builds confidence. As children return to Millbrook across different books, they recognise the people and places. This lets them focus on new concepts rather than adjusting to new worlds.

Connected stories reinforce learning. Characters grow, their understanding deepens, and economic concepts layer naturally.

Real community dynamics teach systems thinking. Millbrook functions as a real community where actions have ripple effects.

Diverse perspectives enrich understanding. The Millbrook Crew come from different backgrounds and bring different strengths. Jamal's analytical thinking complements Connor's hands-on resourcefulness. Maya's leadership balances Lily's empathy. Children see that there are multiple valid approaches to economic challenges.

From Story to Understanding

The magic happens in the gap between reading and reflection. Children finish a chapter thinking about friendship, fairness, and problem-solving. They're not consciously aware they just learned about incentive structures or marginal analysis. But they did.

Later, when they encounter a similar situation in real life, something clicks. The patterns they observed in Millbrook help them make sense of their own experiences. The economic concepts have moved from abstract principles to practical tools.

This is embedded learning. Knowledge that becomes part of how children see the world, not just facts they memorise for tests.

The Millbrook Town Adventures Series

The Millbrook Kid's Fair is the first of the series. Each book introduces core economic concepts through connected adventures featuring the Millbrook Crew.

Other books explore how money works and why saving matters, how to manage budgets and make smart financial decisions, how people produce things and why trade benefits everyone, how prices guide decisions and markets coordinate activity, what governments do and why we need public services, and what makes communities prosperous over time. Together they build a comprehensive foundation in economic and financial literacy across Key Stage 2 and 3.

For younger readers, our Key Stage 1 picture books introduce foundational concepts through the same Millbrook setting with age-appropriate stories and illustrations.

Visit Millbrook Town

Head to www.millbrooktown.co.uk to:

- Discover all the books in the series
- Access additional activities and discussion guides
- Stay updated on new Millbrook adventures

MILLBROOK
TOWN

Printed in Dunstable, United Kingdom

77955621R00078